Sex,

MW01484165

. . . .

"'There are no maps or guidebooks,' Alexia LaFortune writes as she begins the 'tales of womanhood' that drive this memoir's journey into the feminine. Yet she maps the landmarks of her inner geography like a seasoned navigator. The trek is personal, spiritual, universal, and utterly human. At once self-assured and self-conscious, LaFortune traverses the highlands, flatlands, and wetlands of love, heartache, insecurity, and faith, ultimately proving there is no better life-guide than the wisdom of experience. More than a map, this book is a beautiful, selfless offering from mother to daughter. Baring heart and soul, exposing her innermost secrets, LaFortune imparts the greatest gift of all—the gift of knowing that every mother's and daughter's journey is a shared one.

—CARMELLA PADILLA, author of *The Work of Art: Folk Artists in the 21st Century* and *El Rancho de las Golondrinas: Living History in New Mexico's La Cienega Valley.*

"How Susan Doherty became Alexia LaFortune is a beautifully written memoir that will make you grateful to be a woman and more open to the possibilities that magic exists in our everyday lives. Written as a love letter to her daughter, it's the kind of book you wish you'd had been given along with your Girl Scout manual and Emily Post."

—PATRICIA MORRISROE, author of *9 ½ Narrow: My Life in Shoes*

"Read this book to remember your own youthful romances. Read this book to watch a woman carve her chosen path, and to witness the gift of story—in all its elegant and naked beauty—laid at her daughter's feet. Women, read this book and see yourself."

—LISA DALE NORTON, author of *Hawk Flies Above: Journey to the Heart of the Sandhills* and *Shimmering Images: A Handy Little Guide to Writing a Memoir*

"I couldn't put this book down. It dug in deep and wouldn't let go. It's a stunning read. A love letter from mother to a daughter, and truthfully, it's for all daughters, all our daughters. It's filled with messy, gorgeous, heartbreaking, and heart-cracking truth. The thing about great writing, bold writing is this: It stays with you. Hounds you. Haunts you. Awakens you. Lingers with you. Alexia LaFortune is a great writer. This is a great book. I couldn't put it down, and I didn't want it to end."

—AMY FERRIS, author of *Marrying George Clooney: Confessions from a Midlife Crisis*

"What if you weren't a movie star, but you had a pretty rollicking life? And what if you were willing, for the sake of your soul and that of your daughter's, to spill the raw truth of your life, part secret and part sacred? This memoir of Alexia LaFortune's is that book. *Sex, Love, and Spirit* brings a life forged in the wild '60s and '70s to baby boomers of all ages. It's a good read, a reunion with self, and doesn't let us down."

—JOAN LOGGHE, Santa Fe Poet Laureate Emerita

"This is a necessary book, an important book, and except for the fact that it is memoir it is reminiscent of the 'new feminist literature' that was fictionalized by the likes of Marilyn French, Marge Piercy, and Rita Mae Brown back in the day. This one is for all the boomer girls who loved the bad boys and the wounded birds and especially for the ones who have daughters to warn. If you lived—really lived—through the last half of this century, you will relate to this memoir with the deepest nostalgia. If you were in a convent or under a rock somewhere, you will see what you missed out on."

—Corie Skolnick, author of *ORFAN* and *America's Most Eligible*

"From the first words—'Mummy said I wandered but I was looking for the light'—this book had me in its thrall and I could not put it down. Breathless, I cheered Alexia LaFortune's restless journey from man to man to soulmate; from heartbreak to love; from lost to found. LaFortune is a spiritual seeker who writes with elegance and wit. Her dialogue is exquisite, her writing is, in turn, lyrical, sexy, hilarious, and always deeply honest. This deep and important tome from a mother to a daughter glows with authentic tales of womanhood that made me want to tell my own tales to my daughter. Her lyrical prose inspired me to dig deeper as a writer. What a poetess! What a woman!"

—Linda Schreyer, author of *Tears and Tequila* and TV screenwriter

"Reading Alexia LaFortune's *Sex, Love, and Spirit* reminded me of all the challenges women faced during the years before the women's movement really took off. She relates stories that often left me with my mouth hanging open in surprise and sometimes laughing out loud. LaFortune's memoir is a wonderful examination of what it means to live a courageous life. Thanks to her candor, humor, and warmth, her memoir actually lives up to the title, and you find that you won't be able to put it down."

—Renee Swindle, author of *Shake Down the Stars* and *A Pinch of Ooh La La*

"The authenticity and openness Alexia LaFortune pours into each page feels more like an intimate exchange with a lifelong friend than a memoir intended for large audiences. She, the girl, the daughter, the woman, traveling to and with her own beloved daughter, reminds me of the common threads that connect women. While we are not all mothers, we are all daughters, and that job title comes with undeniable similarities. You will come to love this author, and you will certainly see yourself in her journey."

—KRISTINE VAN RADEN, coauthor of *Letters to Our Daughters*

"Alexia weaves a compelling journey into divine feminine consciousness, lived through and told as we all find it—in glimpses, fits and starts, stumbles backward and leaps forward, unanswerable questions, and gifts from the Earth. This is a book that many will relate to in its struggle between the pull of the spiritual unknown and the messy reality of the physical present."

—TANYA TAYLOR RUBINSTEIN, CEO, Global School of Story

Sex, Love, and *Spirit*

Pat —

New friend, gracias!
Love,
Alexia

Sex, Love
and Spirit

a memoir

Alexia LaFortune

The Thunder, Perfect Mind

For I am the first and the last.
I am the wife and the virgin.
I am the mother and the daughter.
I am she whose wedding is great.
And I have not taken a husband . . .

For I am knowledge and ignorance.
I am shame and boldness.
I am shameless; I am ashamed.
I am strength and I am fear.
I am war and I am peace.

—*Gnostic poem dating from the first century* A.D.

Published 2016
Printed in the United States of America
ISBN: 978-0-9974462-0-3
e-ISBN: 978-0-9974462-1-0
Library of Congress Control Number: 2016905632

Cover and interior design by Tabitha Lahr
Cover art, DIVINUS by Greg Spalenka

For permission requests and information, please address:
Alexia LaFortune
tonantzinpress@gmail.com
www.alexialafortune.com

"In the tradition of Celtic storytelling, scenes have been conflated, personages composited, names changed – all to tell an honest tale."

The more a daughter knows the details of her mother's life—without flinching or whining—the stronger the daughter.

—Anita Diamant, *The Red Tent*

Los Angeles, 2000

I was taking my daughter to college.

It had been two years since we moved to L.A., and I still felt as if I'd been banished, exiled to the Bastille, from Santa Fe, New Mexico. Santa Fe is my religion, where I feel most blessed. I had to discover its beauty, but when I did, beauty reigned. It became my home for seventeen years, the place that nourished the life I always dreamed of finding. A place where the layering of ordinary days—marriage, raising a child, building a home with the support of a multicultural community— were lived out like a fiesta. *Que viva!*

When my husband, Greg, a builder, turned fifty, he longed for something new—new vision, new challenges. He claimed that if he had to build another faux adobe *casa*, we'd have to bury him in it. I loved him. We headed west.

The move was hard on our daughter, Vanessa; it was hard to leave the only home she had ever known, her *compadres*. At first L.A. was exciting, yet soon she was lost, became self-conscious that she wasn't really a So Cal kind of girl. The ensuing months brought the Big Breakup with the guy back home, some futile crushes, and a whole lot of loneliness.

I, too, became bereft without my house and land, the red earth and luminous sky, my dear friends, my seasonal rituals— and I never expected that the "change of life" would actually come in and completely *change my life.* I wrote screenplays, assuming a supreme reason for being in L.A. other than playing the supportive wife. Though after a year pitching my chick flicks to disinterested twenty-five-year-old industry boys, I became embarrassed to be a fifty-year-old woman. I truly doubted whether I had *anything* worthwhile to say.

We rented an apartment in an upscale neighborhood of Santa Monica that cost double our Santa Fe mortgage and came with with fleas, rats, and a landlady who asked, "What? You never had small animals in your house before?" A young home-less man took up residence in my open-garage parking space, pissing, vomiting, and spitting out angry curses.

And now, my sweet child, whose very existence kept me teth-ered and gave my life meaning, was in deep need of my assurance. Greg was busy, thriving in his career with a design/build firm.

We barreled south down the 405. Maybe not exactly *barrel-ing* compared to the rest of the traffic whizzing past us. It took every molecule of my being to drive that car. I white-knuckled the wheel, gritted my teeth, and tried to keep up with the speed limit and avoid a complete meltdown. I was that close.

The morning began with an earthquake, my first, roaring in like a locomotive, jolting me awake, then cramps, a sinus head-ache, and a sizzling blister of a sun. All of which was not why I was a wreck. I had been well on my way to completely losing it before this day arrived, but now this morning was turning out to be the one that might swift-kick me over the edge.

I risked a brief glance next to me. My girl sat scrunched up against the door. She was silent, difficult to read. Her honey hair was beachy thick and long. She twirled a silky strand, dressed in the de rigueur cut-off shorts and tank top. Her flip flops were kicked off her tiny feet. Unlike me, of Irish amazon heritage, she was petite, characteristic of her father's French family. Although her skin glowed Eire ivory, like moonstone.

"You okay, Ness?" Her usual composure could be deceptive.

She took a swig from her bottled water and swallowed. "I don't like change."

Given her experience over the past two years, why should she?

"But, sweetie, what if change means, 'Thank God! I'm glad *that's* over'?"

"Hmm, yeah, I guess," she said. "What if it doesn't, though? What if it's the Big Bad?"

"Vanessa, *mija*, as much as I would love to keep you forever curled up next to me watching reruns of *Buffy* . . ." Then I wanted to say, yes, what if? Let's go back! There are vampires out there!

"I know it's time we both went out and met new people." Her tone was mocking but there was a world of hope behind the flatness: *Right, Mama?*

She slid in a CD, some folk-rock Celtic group. We continued hurtling down the freeway, racing against the pounding thunder of the music and our own heartbeats.

This was not going well. Where were my words of wisdom to pull her through? How could I urge her to trust her life and its unfolding, to love life and the changes it brings, the fallow and the full, when she sees me thrashing and unsure? How could I locate my faith and pass the truth of it on to her, when the overwhelming elements of my own circumstances at this time obscured it?

I wanted her to know that she will break through isolation; that she will survive shame and overcome failure; and that heartbreak is not fatal. I wanted her to know that she is connected to something vast and powerful, beautiful and sacred.

Vanessa reached over, turned down the volume on a particularly hard-thumping reel. Thank God.

"Mama, whatever happened between you and that musician?"

"What do you mean? Are you asking why it didn't work out?"

"Yeah, I mean, I know you love Daddy and all that, but an Irish bodhran player seems so cool."

"Yup, cool." *Crap, I can't do this now. Well, you see, Ness, it was like this: He was married.* "Just one of those things, baby. Didn't work out."

I signaled for the next exit.

"Oh, jeez, Mama! What if I can't do this?"

What could I say? I needed to know that myself.

* * *

In the weeks that followed, with Vanessa gone and struggling to settle into dorm life, too many of my hours were logged wondering, *What's the point?* My downward spiral eclipsed the quotidian boundaries of my Los Angeles depression.

Since our move, Greg had been urging me to accompany him to the Self-Realization Shrine in the Pacific Palisades. He had found solace there over the past several decades on his occasional visits to Southern California.

He described his experiences at the temple by the sea. "I always hear the one thing I need, some nugget of a message that I can carry away with me."

I hadn't been able to rouse myself to attend the services that he and Vanessa had sometimes enjoyed together. I was still angry with the gods for screwing me and sending me to this soulless hellhole.

Feeling especially desperate one Sunday morning, I asked Greg to take me to the Shrine.

A steep but narrow waterfall rippled the lake's surface. On the far side, two swans emerged from the tall grasses, gliding toward the center. We followed a curving path through lush tropical vegetation, and we came upon a fern-filled spacious grotto, where a stone bust of the Madonna and Child rested at the entrance. I had become fond of the images of the Lady of Guadalupe so prevalent in Santa Fe, had my own collection, but I didn't expect to see this visage of the divine displayed here amongst Hindu deities. Her presence was a familiar blessing: *I'm still here, wherever you are.* Why do I keep forgetting? Gratitude, like a cleansing breath, loosened the iron grip of my fear, silenced the remonstrative voice demanding the continuance of the illusion that my life be a certain way. Greg held my gaze with his usual expression of calm approval. Always approving of me, my husband was. Always true. The current of our connection passed through me, deepened to the locus, the vital place where our love had taken root so many years ago. *This is what's real.* The circular latticed canopy of the grotto was open, spoked like a medicine wheel. A breeze rustled the trees. I exhaled, breathed into the expansive beauties of the universe. Inhaled eros, with everything.

Later I dream I am lying on a table crafted of slender branches. A seasoned crone, her dark skin creased like a pecan, touches my body, as if anointing it, with greenery, leaves, and herbs. She doesn't speak, but I hear her voice just the same: *Now that you have been blessed in nature's beauty, as in fact you have always been, trust your way, reveal your truths.* At once I am standing. Pink rose petals gush from inside my clothing. I remove handful upon handful as they flutter through the air, pungent with the scent of possibility, the aroma of life itself.

Her final words echo through my wonder: *Remember, the unspoken can always be written.*

I awaken, write:

Mija, Vanessa, mi corazon,

As you go out into the world, out of your mother's house, as I deliver you to the waiting arms of others, I realize there is more I must tell you, take you to places not easily shared by a mother and daughter.

These are my tales of womanhood. I hope they will help you find your way. Make you stronger. There are no maps or guidebooks. The way of the feminine is to descend into the mysterious, discovering the light in the darkness. From there you are launched.

You came to us through love, but there were shadows. I broke the rules.

Yet what I never doubted was the rightness of your father and me being together. We both knew. Still do.

Know this: I confess but do not seek absolution. Every stunning step, the sins, the lamentations, and the exaltations, all brought me to you. The stories that follow, my tales of sex, love, and spirit, evoked in part by your own questions and in large measure by my own, are also for you. May they help you dispel your doubts and insecurities, regrets and fears, as you discover at once yourself and the illusion of separation.

Boston, 1950s

....

I was born on March 22, 1950. My mother exclaimed that my head looked like an orange. Daddy said, "You have your son, now I have my daughter." I was christened Susan Dorothy Doherty. The name change came later.

* * *

Mummy said I wandered, but I knew I was looking for the light. Knew it was out there. And I was young—maybe three, four years old. She would hang a sign around my neck, Do Not Feed, and off I'd go into the next yard, around the block, even miles away. Sometimes a neighbor would find me. Often the police. Mummy would give me a lickin', but still I'd roam. So she tied me, with a long rope around my waist, to the chain-link fence around our backyard. I caught the tip of my nose on that fence, cut it on the top wire as I tried to climb over.

Still, she tried to contain me. I called out to the boy next door, Fatty Francis, to please come untie me. He was short, but good with knots. I then led him by the hand to the cliff at the end of our property, and we started climbing. Higher and higher, I climbed. When I heard Francis bawling, I looked back. He was stuck and scared.

Mummy came running, shouting, "Don't move! Stay right there!"

But I was afraid of the wallop I'd get when she got to me, so I turned over on my stomach and slid all the way down. When I got to the bottom, I had a mouthful of dirt and a chipped front tooth.

* * *

When I was six we moved. Mummy had a new baby and a big house to take care of, so I was free to roam. But this time I was really lost and it was getting dark. I was already lost so bad that when I got home, I was gonna get it. Mummy always said I got more spankings than the two boys put together. When that didn't work she gave me a dose of phenobarbital so she could get some rest. She's not naughty, she'd tell Daddy, just active, won't take a nap.

And now these tough girls had my bike, had pushed me right off, and wouldn't give it back. That could mean the belt when Daddy got home.

Daddy had just taken off the training wheels on Saturday. I had practiced riding all weekend.

"Stay on the sidewalk," Dad said, "in front of the house."

"Can I just go to the end of the block?"

"You heard me. No."

After school on Monday, I couldn't wait to go for a ride. "Don't go too far," Mummy said as I headed out the door. "Remember what your father told you."

But I wanted to show off my two-wheeler to Laura, my new

best friend, who had a cat and watched *American Bandstand*. She lived around the corner, on Tremlett Hill. Surely Daddy hadn't meant I was to stay in front of the house forever. However, Laura wasn't home. So I walked my bike back up the steep incline, and instead of turning into my street, I wheeled it around, hopped back on, raised my feet off the pedals, and flew down the hill.

Skipper, my big brother, had let me ride inside his scooter, an orange crate fastened to a roller skate, and we'd screamed down Tremlett. But it didn't compare to being on my own, the wind filling my lungs with big gulps of *freeeeeeeee!*

When I reached the bottom of the hill, I had kept on going.

* * *

"It's a damn stupid bike," said one of the tough girls.

"It's a baby's bike," said the skinny one, even meaner.

Then she slapped me, hard on the face. She slapped me again and again and again until I cried, and she sang, "Baby! Boo-hoo! Look at the little ba-by!"

Then some big boy was there. "Hey, kid," he said, "you wanna know a secret?"

I thought he felt sorry for me, so I nodded yes and tried to stop my tears.

"Do you know how babies are made?" he asked me, smiling at the tough girls.

"No," I said, sniffling. I'd never thought about it. And I didn't care. All I wanted was to be out of there.

He leaned in close, the girls laughing, while he whispered in my ear, "The man sticks his thing into a woman." He pointed at me "down there." My first-grade teacher, Sister Hellarian, who pulled my hair every time she walked by me, said we should *never* touch ourselves "down there." This boy was wrong.

They all were laughing so hard that the skinny one lost her balance and fell off the curb. Now this made the other two go hysterical. "Shut up!" she shrieked, "I hurt myself." She was trying not to cry. "I gotta go." The other girl threw down my bike, called after her friend, "Paula!"

The boy was already walking away, picking his big, fat, stupid-head nose.

Now I had to find my way home. I pumped like the dickens to get out of there, but after a few blocks, when I saw Melville Avenue up ahead, I knew I was okay and closer than I thought. Straight up Melville, then right on Hooper. Sometimes Skipper and I took this route after school. He was the line-patrol guy, got to wear a white belt with a silver badge across his chest, made Laura and me walk silently behind him. Even after we dropped Laura off, he insisted I follow single file behind him all the way home. I made faces behind his back, stuck out my bum and did a hootchie-kootchie dance.

The bad thing about Melville, though, was the Witch's house. A humongous, grungy, purple house set way back from the street. Every other house along the avenue was pretty and neat, with trimmed front lawns and clipped hedges. I'd never seen the Witch—Mummy said it didn't look like *anyone* lived in the house, it was such an overgrown dump—but Skipper said the Tobin twins had seen her plenty of times. He said he also knew who threw the stones that broke her front windows, but he wasn't telling. The house looked so dark and empty when I got to it, I was thinking Mum was probably right, and maybe she would like it if I brought her some of these lilacs spilling over the sidewalk. Maybe then she wouldn't be so mad. I tried to yank a branch off real quick while still straddling my bike, but the branches bent like rubber. A shower of blossoms sprinkled on my head and shoulders. I was brushing them off when the Witch came *flying* out of her front

22

door, yelling her head off. Too scared to move, I just stood there as she ran toward me. Then she stopped and we both just stood there together, the world silent, her eyes, deep pools. I struggled in their wavy surface, caught in the undertow. I became numb, sure that every bit of what kept me alive was being sucked right out.

An orange cat pounced on her railing. Another tumbled and stretched in the weeds. Her eyes twitched, lost their grip.

"I have cats," I blurted. "They're not really mine, but sometimes I find them. My mother won't let them in the house, so I keep them in the garage. No one ever goes in there. Sometimes me and Laura brush their teeth, dress them up, tie them in my doll carriage, and take them for walks." I could see my words, a thin stream floating before me. The letters lifted, floated, curved around her, then dipped, swallowed by those eyes. "Skipper says if you drop a cat, even from our second-floor porch, it'll land on its feet, I mean, paws. I haven't tried that yet."

The Witch swallowed, blinked, returned from somewhere far away. Was she deciding what evil she would do to me? Or was she just thinking about cats? I sucked in the lilac-scented air and blinked right back at her.

"People look at me," she said. Her not-yelling voice was small. She didn't even sound old, not like my Nana. She was the youngest old person I had ever seen. For sure, the wildest. But not nearly as scary as Sister Hellarian. "They look in my windows. They want to take me away."

"Oh," I said, nodding but not understanding.

"Will you help me?"

"Okay." But I felt bad that she thought I was her friend when all I wanted was to be away from her.

"Do you want to come inside?" she asked. The orange cat curled around her legs, pushing up the skirt of her long black dress. Underneath I could see her gray socks, thick like the kind Skipper wore in winter. They were all holey, though, and smushed down around her ankles. But she had on red sneakers just like mine, except hers were dirty and didn't have any laces.

"I guess I could, for a little bit," I told her.

Before following her to the back of the house, I looked around, hoping someone, *anyone*, might see me, but the neighborhood was empty. The windows of the houses looked back at me as if holding their breath.

The path was narrow and bushy. I pushed my bike through, not wanting to let it out of my sight, scratching my legs against the thorny stems of gigunda roses. I had never seen such roses. They crawled up thick ropey vines along the foundation leading to broken, slanty steps. The back porch sagged under the collected weight of tons of stuff. Just rusty old junk, Mummy would say. Yellowed, brown-stained newspapers were jammed into the cracked windows. The Witch pushed open the back door, and one of the cats bolted inside. Then she turned to me, her eyes black and shiny. A sudden breeze lifted her long white hair like a whip across her wrinkly face.

I could not go in that house.

"I'll be right back!" I yelled, and I raced home lickity-split.

* * *

I parked my bike in the garage, grateful that at least I had beat Daddy home. And then, Mummy was so busy getting dinner ready and feeding Edward that she just glanced at me with her *I'm at my wits end* look as I came through the kitchen door.

"You okay?"

"I'm tired. I should've joined a convent." She wiped a wet cloth across Edward's moon face smeared with Gerber's. "Look at you," she said to me. "You're grubby. Go wash up."

"Okay . . . But Mummy, where do old people go?"

"If they've been good, they go to heaven."

"But what about before heaven?"

"Miami," she said. "That's where I'm going."

* * *

Terrified, I couldn't sleep. There was a Witch with shiny eyes mad at me. And the Boogeyman! He might climb the front hall stairs and do to me what that big boy told me. I had never seen a grown man thing, but I knew I didn't want him sticking it into me.

I got out of bed. Mummy won't like it, bare feet on the cold floor, but I couldn't take the time to put on my slippers. I had to find her.

She was in the kitchen, talking on the phone. I climbed on her lap, clasped my arms tightly around her neck. I could not stop crying.

"What's wrong with you?"

"Don't let me go, Mummy. Please don't let me go."

"Yes, yes, all right . . . Sorry, Nora," she said into the receiver . . . "No, working late again. I swear I went from a domineering mother to a domineering husband . . . What? . . . Oh, I know. It's a miracle I survived the winter. Next year, I am definitely going to Miami."

Mummy, please don't leave me.

"Honey, you're squeezing my neck. Oh for heaven's sake, Susan. Now that's enough, go to bed."

"Please, hold me!"

"Bed," she said, giving me a shove.

I sprinted through the dark house, my fingers plugging my ears, humming to ward off the dangers of night, *la, la, la*. A slash of light leaked into the hall from the bottom of Skipper's closed door. When I reached my room, the statue of the Blessed Mother, whose mild features I had dolled up with crayons, glowed in the dark. I could hear Edward's sleeping milky breath in the crib next to my bed, smell the newness of him. I leapt under the covers, my back to the windows, spooked by the sinister slats of the venetian blinds, the slices of street light. My fists balled, pressed up against my chest, as tears gathered again.

But then, a thought, like a strong, safe caress, a robust *knowing* wriggled through the sharp, salty keening. My body unfolded, my soul opened in prayer, heard the promise of salvation: Miami. Mummy would go to her Ami. When I grew up, I would go to mine. My own special place, my Ami.

The Good Shepherd

···

Dad called Father Scanlon "a sport." He said this with a shake of his head and with more than a hint of bemused disbelief. To me Father Scanlon was a star, glamorous, tooling about the parish in his red convertible.

Father Scanlon had a penchant for good scotch with his lobster thermidor. He turned up at the best restaurants, Dini's or Jimmy's Harborside, a guest of the Irish Catholic "pols" who greeted their cronies wielding fat cigars and portentous handshakes. Dad said Father had the direct line to God as well as Mayor Curley.

Week nights he showed up for cocktails and supper at any one of a number of parishioners' homes eager for his blessing. Most often, by seven thirty, he knelt in the living room of Doctor Foley, his Wednesday golf date, leading the doctor's family, his wife and nine kids, in the rosary. Teresa Foley was in my fourth-grade class, as was Lumpy Liam, her older brother who had been kept back. When Father Scanlon dropped in for his monthly religion quizzes, he called each of the Foleys by nicknames: Sis and Buddy.

I was jealous.

Mum didn't like me playing with the Foleys. Said they were hooligans, no polish. But I longed to be invited for fish sticks and orangeade and then the rosary like the other lucky kids who befriended them.

Why, I wondered, didn't Father Scanlon ever come to our house?

"I don't know, for sure," answered Mummy. "Daddy doesn't like him, thinks he's a show-off. And Daddy should know, he knows all the big shots. He even writes speeches for Senator Jack Kennedy." She sniffed, lifted her nose a bit in the air.

I guessed Mummy liked the Kennedys, dressing up in her mink stole after sugaring her face with powder and lipstick before "attending a tea," she said, with those Kennedy sisters.

"Is Daddy a big shot?"

"Ha! He thinks so, big-shot attorney. All his promises, said I'd live like a queen. I'm sure Lady *Jacqueline* doesn't have to scrub the kitchen floor."

Or maybe we just weren't holy enough.

So I practiced my devout looks in the bathroom mirror, memorized my catechism until I could recite the questions and answers with perfection. I knelt on the floor beside my bed, reciting the rosary with grave intonations of piety. I droned on and on until my knees burned and I could no longer swallow my yawns. I gave up desserts, dropped my penny candy money in the poor box, even though it wasn't Lent.

When Father Scanlon came to class again, the atmosphere grew heady within the web of our devotion. He called on his regulars, ignored me in the back, my right arm arrow-straight and reaching, fingers waving in salute, piercing the air. The minutes passed; my intentions were ignored.

I put my arm down. Became still.

I beheld my priest. Fixed him with my light.

He found me. Winked. Called me "Cookie"!

* * *

The morning Sister announced that Father Scanlon wished to see me in the office, my curious classmates scoured me for telling signs of exceptional distinction of which heretofore none of us had been aware. I glanced at Teresa, who ignored me and my sudden attention. When I sauntered down the aisle, I preened, a *special* child of God.

Father Scanlon was alone, slumped behind Sister Superior's desk as well as he could in the inflexible hardness of her straight wooden chair, staring out the high windows at the vacant white sky. He sat in shadow, appeared smaller, even slight, as if it was only the presence of our attention that made him so much bigger.

"Good morning, Father."

He straightened to face me, cleared his throat, and reentered himself, his eyes alight. "Hi there, Cookie!" he said, just like we were old pals. "Come on in and shut the door."

"Yes, Father." *Yes, indeed-y!* I clicked the door closed, stood before the desk, my smile and posture attesting to the excitement of my proud good fortune.

"Boy!" he exclaimed. "You're a big one, aren't you!

Oh.

"We're going to have to put a dictionary on your head, weigh you down, so you don't grow anymore."

"Yes, Father, I . . . I'm tall for my age." But it always surprised me, because, actually, I barely felt like I was seen at all.

"Come around here. Let me look at you up close . . . That's a girl. Gee, pretty soon you won't be able to fit on my lap, will you?"

I giggled, flushed. "No, Father, I guess I won't."

"Well, how 'bout now?" he joked, patting his thigh.

"You mean like Santa Claus? I'm already too big for that!"

"Awe, come on, let's give it a try. Ready to come on board?"

He extended his arm, welcoming. Hesitant, I scrunched to shrink, pretend smaller, my hands clasped low in front of me. I inched forward. His arm circled around my back, drawing me close beside him. I leaned, tilting into him. An affectionate hug.

My priest loves me!

His hand slid down, cupping my bum, lingered.

I stiffened, instinctively hopping back beyond his reach, my own hand springing to replace his touch.

"Oh," he said, pressing his palms together as though in prayer. "Excuse me. I didn't know you were so sensitive."

"Yes, Father," I nodded, thick in my confusion.

"You can go back to class now."

But I didn't, stayed in the girls' bathroom, locked and hidden in the last stinky stall, shivering against the cold tile. I waited until the lunch bell rang, joined the others lining up in the hall. Falling in behind Teresa Foley, I marched into the auditorium, took my place, knelt before one of the metal chairs, whose seats served as our makeshift trays, and stuffed down my bologna sandwich.

The Gates to Hell

I t is pelting and I am nine, soaked in my thin beige poplin raincoat, standing at the top of a grassy knoll. The new neighborhood stretches below.

* * *

"Your father is finally making money," said Mummy. "I'm finally getting my dream house."

We had moved to Jamaica Plain, on Moss Hill, a sweep of Tudor and Colonial houses, to the crest: a home development of low-slung ranches and split-levels.

"Modernistic," she exclaimed, so very impressed with her custom castle: pale pink Portuguese marble fireplace (boasting to anyone who would listen that she choose each piece herself) in the living room, plum broadloom, rose silk chairs, and ivory sofa. Of course we were never allowed in that room swathed in plastic sheets; it was only "for show," the covers whisked off for Saturday-night grown-up guests, cocktails and cold cuts.

I had my own room, the woodwork fresh and golden, unlike the dark finish in our old house where ugly monster faces sometimes assembled out of the patterns; a four-poster bed; and a window overlooking a giant weeping willow, a tree so roomy, with swooping generous boughs to climb on and play beneath, and tendrils so very thick that could shelter me and Edward even during a sprinkle.

"Third largest tree in Boston," Dad reported. Then again, for so many years, he had fibbed that the scar on his shiny bald head was from a ricochet Japanese bullet. He had been captain of his own ship in the war, so I tended to believe him. That was until Skip whispered it wasn't true. Dad had just gotten it from playing football when he was a kid.

* * *

There was no such shelter here. I surveyed the expansive view. Droplets of water clung to the sloping blades, sparkling like fairy dust. The meek sun attempted to break through, the droplets holding rainbows, whole worlds of tiny delight. A gust roared in, tearing my flame-hued umbrella from my numb clench. I let the wind take it, watched in wonder as it sailed spinning to the bottom of the hill. I followed its trail, ran down, back to the top. I let it fly once more. And again and again. Joy.

My elation soured. I swallowed back volleys of fear as I climbed the stairs to the back door of the school. The bell had rung; I was late. This new school was bright, not like the dungeon of Saint Mark's. Instead of heavy veils, the nuns wore starched white origami sails—birds of prey or peace was yet to be revealed. Sister Celeste, the principal, was waiting, smiling. I grinned back in relief.

I tried to slide past her into the shadowed vestibule, "Good Morning, Sister."

She swooped in, a flapping vulture, snatched my folded, soggy umbrella.

"You're late!" she shrieked, striking me with it on the shoulder—splattering wet nylon and metal.

"Sister, I . . . I."

"I was watching you! Playing! Lured by Satan when you're supposed to be in class. We don't behave like that in this school, young lady."

More blows—thwack! Back, head, rump.

"You have to learn! Not in my school!"

* * *

That night, I went to my mother, to apologize. I was kept after school, face to the wall, kneeling on Sister Celeste's office floor, reciting the rosary, my own set—the smooth pink tiny globes eclipsed in the dark corner—while I pondered my misconduct. Sister Celeste had phoned my mother. And now she is sad and angry because I am such a bad girl.

"Don't tell, Daddy, okay?" I whisper. "I promise I'll be good." She's heard it before.

* * *

A whisper to my left—

"Ptht, Thuthan!"

"Huh?"

"Thit up," Carrie lisped. I loved watching the way her rosy

round tongue slipped in and out between her teeth. "You're gonna get in trouble."

"All riigghhtt!" I put down my book, *Gone With The Wind*, hidden inside my catechism. Tried to listen.

Sister Mary George was a mystery to me. She was even kind of pretty. Except she had that walk, all stuck-up, like she knew it. And a mean, closed-up face. Never smiled. Not once. Never. I wondered if the other nuns liked her. Maybe she was just sad that she had to be a nun.

"Jesus was brought to the temple for the Circumcision," she said.

My hand shot up. "Just what was the Circumcision, Sister?"

Silence.

I honestly didn't know.

To my left, Moose Mulligan, his hand strategically covering his mouth, snickered, "Way to go, Stretch."

To my right, Carrie, her hands neatly folded on her desk, rolled her eyes.

Mary George flushed crimson, crooking her finger inside her stiff white bib like she couldn't breathe and was about to explode. I didn't know what I had done but I knew I was sure in for it.

"Outside, Miss Doherty! Now!"

In the hall, I stood before her, eye to eye.

"Where I come from, you wicked girl, *blah, blah, blah* . . ."

Timothy O'Reilly came out of his eighth-grade classroom. He was so cute. No, he was handsome. And tall. Taller than me. Not like the shrimps in my class. He looked like a movie star. Clark Gable. Even the ears.

Scarlett O'Hara was not beautiful, but men seldom realized it when caught by her charm . . . I could do charm, I thought. Maybe.

Here he comes. No, don't smile! Candy Covello told me getting braces would look cool. They don't.

"Pay attention to me, Miss Doherty. I see where your eyes are wandering," Mary George continued. "And, from now on, you will sit up straight, like a lady, your skirt covering your knees, your legs together, and close those gates to hell!"

WHAT? Did Timothy hear that? I could die.

"You will now take yourself to Sister Celeste's office."

There's more?

The halls were quiet, the floors so polished I practiced walking into my footsteps. At the top of the stairs, there was a vase of plastic yellow roses in front of the statue of Mary. Her arms outstretched, she looked at me like she was saying, "In trouble again? How could you?" *Don't know. Maybe it's cause I'm tall and easy to spot. Candy Covello, who's short, never gets caught. Drats. But maybe Timothy O'Reilly was sent to the principal's office, too, and we'll be like these two bad kids together, and I'll say something neat and he'll see that I'm not just some finky seventh grader.*

Sister Celeste was diminutive but rotund, like she was overstuffed. She waddled; her walk and talk seemed purposefully slow. Her face was porcine, pale and puffy. Her eyes, slitty.

I hated her.

I was going to hell.

Timothy O'Reilly not here, either. Only the scarred and bloody body of Christ hanging on the crucifix.

"You had a boy-girl party?" Sister Celeste asked, like I had done something truly horrid.

"Yes, Sister."

My mother had come up with the idea—a Roaring Twenties party for my birthday in our newly paneled rec room. I invited the whole class, first time, girls and boys both. The girls dressed up like flappers. Candy Covello wore makeup. Only the girls danced. Then Carrie and Dickie Foley, on a dare, did this crazy Charleston. But nothing, well, *boy-girl*, happened. Bobby Spazzi did laugh so hard he barfed up hot dogs and orange tonic. But that was the only bad thing.

"Was there dancing?" Sister Celeste continued.

"Yes, Sister."

"And just what did your parents think of that, *dirty girl*?"

Mum had spent the next week exclaiming, "What a mess! Today I found another bun behind the couch!" Yet when we watched the home movies that Daddy took, she laughed and laughed and said, "What a good party."

"I think they liked it," I said.

"Oh, really? Well, just what would they think of this?"

My stomach rolled. Although I was much taller than Sister Celeste, she could still get to me. She held up a composition I wrote, "My Ideal," waving the papers in my face.

In class, all the other kids had written about their ideal being some saint. Even a few martyrs made it, but especially Jesus and Mary. The Blessed Mother and her Son outnumbered all the others. Please, please, I prayed, don't call on me. How could I have thought mine might be a good idea? I had written about myself, that my ideal person was my best self. My turn came, and Mary George made me stand in the front. I read. Then, I cried. Cause I knew, without even looking up, I knew, without anyone saying a word, that I should be ashamed.

"Kneel down," Sister Celeste ordered, removing a wooden metal-edged ruler from inside the folds of her robe. "Palms out." Then she struck, and struck again, red welts rising to purple, until the tears began to pool at my knees.

"Now go to the chapel and pray to God for humility," she hissed, like she just didn't know what to make of me.

Eden

....

It was the fall of eighth grade, and Jack Connelly, who, all through grammar school, had been a pipsqueak, had shot up over the summer. During recess he was now more interested in girls than in ball games. He gave first kisses to the popular, pretty, and *short* girls. I never even liked Jack—especially how his head looked like a snake, the way it lifted all long and jutty-outy on his neck. However, when he fixed me with his "I'm interested" stare, I didn't care about all that. I knew I wanted mine. A kiss. Even if it had to be Jack's. At least he was tall.

It happened on a Sunday in March. Carrie and I were circling the ice rink in our royal blue stretch pants and matching parkas, when Moose Mulligan skated by, shouting, "Jack wants to meet you out back!"

"Me?" I said, feigning surprise.

Jack had spent most of Friday turned around in his desk, resting his snaky head on his hand and giving me the stare. Whenever I'd look up, he'd smile and nod real slow as if we both shared some secret. After school, while I waited by the third-grade doorway for Edward, Jack, all casual, strolled by.

"You going skating Sunday?" he asked.

"Oh," I answered, "uh-huh, I guess so."

* * *

"I'll go talk to him," Carrie said before skating off.

I waited in the smelly girls' bathroom, sweltering, while Carrie "brokered the deal." That's what she said. Carrie's mom sold real estate.

I looked in the steamy mirror and tried to tuck the frizzy ends of my hair under my knit hat. My mum insisted on setting my hair in tightly wound pin curls each night. At least I only had to wear my glasses in school to see the blackboard. Because of my *enormous* height, I perpetually had to sit in the back. Candy, a shrimp with silky straight hair, was able to sit up front. Being first in line also secured her position during May processions, the one inevitably chosen to crown the Blessed Mother.

"Honey, you're the model type," my mother would say. "You'll see. You're not the cute type."

I had no idea what she meant. I wanted to be cute.

* * *

"He's going to meet you behind the rink," Carrie said. "I'll hold your skates."

When I left the girl's room, Moose was leaning against the snack bar, a big grin on his giant face.

"Shut up, Moose."

"What? I didn't say anything."

"Fathead."

"Olive Oyl."

It was damp and windy, and my nose started to drip, even though the setting was perfect. The ice rink was built on a hill in Brookline overlooking the Boston skyline where this wealthy man, Larz Anderson, a long time ago, had built his estate. The house was gone, but some cool things remained, like a gazebo and a duck pond and the carriage house that was now a museum for vintage cars.

I walked up the stone steps to the garden. There was a trellis overhead and pearly marble statues of almost-naked Greek gods and goddesses. Jack was waiting.

"You ever kiss before?" he asked.

"No," I said, with a sniff and a quick swipe of my nose on my sleeve.

Then he was in my face! His mouth pressed hard—*Owee! Braces here!*—against mine. I didn't even have a chance to close my eyes. *Wait! I'm not ready! Eww!* His tongue darted quickly in and out. I thought I might gag. I lurched backward like a spaz, awkwardly slipping, but not quite falling, on a patch of ice. He smirked, standing there like he was so *it.*

"You need lessons," he said. "Talk to Candy Covello."

A shiver ran through me. The sky was ashen. I could feel the icy slush on the path seep into the thin soles of my loafers. Candy had told me loafers were neat. I felt silly. In my hasty desire for an early spring, I had not worn boots.

Carrie walked me home.

"That was it?" she asked. She hadn't had her kiss yet. She was saving herself for Richard Beymer. She had seen him in *West Side Story* seven times already.

"Yup, sorry, Carrie, that was it."

I felt bad. She looked so disappointed.

"Gee," she said. "Gross."

* * *

That night Mum was in her bedroom, pinning up her hair, while watching *The Ed Sullivan Show*. When I came in to say good-night, I bent down to kiss her, bypassed her cheek, and, for the first time, smooched her right on the lips. She looked up, startled.

"What was *that*?" she asked.

"I dunno, I just felt like it."

"Well, don't do it again! That's how you pass germs. Don't ever let anyone kiss you on the lips."

In our house, we did not lip kiss.

* * *

In 1963, several girls from our grammar school and neighbor-hood were enrolled in Ursuline Academy in Dedham, for high school. I had been eager to escape into this bigger parochial world, which I soon learned was just as strict, only worse: no boys. Candy and I started ditching Mass on Sundays, trading servings of the Eucharist for raspberry-lime rickies. We sneaked down to Center Street and watched the older kids, townies who went to public school, grew up in triple-deckers. We were espe-cially fascinated by the girls. Girls who had teased-up bleached blonde hair, wore ankle bracelets, and smoked filterless ciga-rettes. Girls who flicked the still-lit butts into the street as they piled into cars with boys with greasy DAs and sideburns. Boys in skinny black pants and white T-shirts, the short sleeves rolled or stashed with a cigarette pack. We were sure they must be hoods.

"Hoods," Candy said. "At least borderlines."

"Where do they go?" I asked.

"They just ride around," Candy said. "Or go parking."

"Oh, right." Like I knew.

"Hey, you want to pierce your ears? My dad's going to do mine." Candy's father was a doctor.

"I don't know. I'll ask my mother. She thinks it's cheap looking. What about blonde streaks? I don't think she would mind that."

My mother started dying my hair when I was about eight years old. "You were a blonde baby. And I don't like dark hair." When the natural auburn roots crept in, capping my crown like a yarmulke, I believed she became chagrined to just let me be. Besides, too much work.

Candy agreed, "We could go get some Clairoxide. That's how you do it."

Candy knew things.

* * *

By sophomore year, she was determined we would have boyfriends. It was time. We scoured the Friday-night dances at Catholic Memorial and Boston College High. The prep-school boys didn't seem interested in me though. Even with my braces off and contacts lenses, I was still tall.

Johnny Sullivan was our paperboy. Not from our hood. Mum said his people were shanty Irish. Not our class. He went to English High, where the dropouts from Latin, my dad's alma mater, ended up. His mother worked at Woolworths. We all knew the jolly lady behind the soda fountain who called us all Dollface. Johnny rode his bike every morning across the Jamaicaway to Pond Street, then up Moss Hill Road, delivering the *Globe*. On Fridays, late in the afternoon, he made the rounds to collect his fees. Too shy to go the front door, I spied on him from behind the drapes of the living-room picture window. I had a wicked crush on him. I was not alone—all the girls on Moss

Hill did, except Candy. She was crazy about Danny Cotter, who liked her back. They had spent the last week on the phone, every night. She came up with a plan.

"I'll just invite Johnny to a party on Saturday night when he comes by Friday with his bill."

"What about your mother?"

"I'll meet him outside. Gawd, you are so mental sometimes."

"Do you think he'll come?"

"Of course, why not?"

"Okay, just don't say I like him or anything."

* * *

True to her word, Candy arranged for me to sleep over. My dad dropped me off, and I let myself in the back door, dropping my blue leather train case on the kitchen table. I paused to listen to the house sounds: muffled giggles and gasps from the den; the deep bass of the Righteous Brothers playing on the hi-fi in the rec room below. *Please God, let him like me!* We had till ten o'clock, Candy said. That's when her parents would be home.

My right hand trembled on the banister as I slowly crept down the stairs. Approaching the open doorway, I wiped both hands on the sides of my cranberry wool culottes, cleared my throat. *I'm such a dork!*

He sat on the orange studio couch. "Hi, I'm Johnny." Just like that, he spoke. But I couldn't reply because of the miracle of John Sullivan before me. Then he said, "That's Martin."

Some brilliantined greaser was inspecting the Covellos' albums. He turned and checked me out.

"You alone?" Martin asked, glancing past me.

"Yes," I squeaked. "Candy's, um, they're, ya know, upstairs."

"Isn't anyone else coming?" Martin was catching on.

"I don't think so."

"I've seen you around," Johnny said to me. His blue oxford cloth shirt matched his eyes; his blonde curls erupted despite whatever he had tried to tone them down with.

"You have?" I couldn't believe it. Something hot and sweet and terrifying somersaulted inside me. "I mean, yeah, me too. You."

Martin slammed a record back in its cardboard sleeve and tossed it. "This is shitty. We thought there was a party. You comin', Sully?"

Johnny looked up at me.

Don't leave! Don't leave! Don't leave!

"No, you can split." Johnny said, "I'm gonna stick around."

* * *

Our make-out marathons began. From the banks of the Jamaica Pond and the tall grasses of Arnold's Arboretum to the alley behind Marshall's Drugstore, any place we could find to be alone. It never bothered me that Johnny didn't talk much. In fact, we shared very little except the eager exploration of each other's bodies.

"Mum, I'm going to confession!" Or "Dad, will you drive me to Carrie's to babysit?" All lies, of course. Some nights I caught my dad, who wouldn't let me date—"Not until you're a senior," he said—on the lookout for me, cruising up Center Street. Johnny and I would slip into the shadows of Saint Thomas Aquinas Church. Pressed into the corners, up against the cold stone walls, we were safe, the faint smell of incense and the chiming of the bells somehow making our kisses, our tender holding, feel hardly like sin at all.

How could God not want me to love this boy? This was the holiest I'd ever felt.

It didn't matter anyway if I was sinning. I was already a lost soul. I had tried to be saved. I had taken the train into Saint Anthony's Shrine in downtown Boston to make my confession. I hadn't been for a while, and at St. Anthony's you could be sure of a quickie. Besides, nobody knew me there. It was also Good Friday, and since I had to attend Mass with my parents on Easter Sunday, they would expect me to receive communion. It was my Catholic duty.

"Bless me, Father, for I have sinned. It's been six months since my last confession, and these are my sins."

"Yes, my child," the priest began, his Irish brogue creaky, ancient. "Go on."

My voice dropped low. "I French kissed my boyfriend."

"You what? Speak up."

Oh, jeez.

"Kissed, Father. I French kissed."

"And just what is this French kiss," he bellowed. "What?"

Yikes!

"With tongues, Father." I could see him through the screen sit up and press his face all twisted toward me like he was going to blow a gasket.

"You are going to end up on the street like those floozies who sell themselves!"

I mean, I knew it was a grievous sin, but I didn't expect this.

"You're no better than a prostitute, a *manky* whore! In the gutter, you'll be," he spat. "The angels are sorrowful weepin'. You're lost, I'm tellin' you, lost!"

"I'm sorry, Father. Yes, Father." I fumbled with the panels of the weighty drapery, feeling for my way out. Not waiting to hear my penance, I had to get out of there, dashing down the aisle despite the tears blurring my exit.

Bless me, Father, for I have sinned. And that was my very last confession.

The Call

....

1967.

First day, first class, first hour, first minutes, in senior home-room, the battle lines were drawn.

"Miss Doherty?"

"Yes, Sister Stigmata?"

"What kind of hairdo is that?"

"Um, a ponytail."

"And you think it's appropriate, do you, for school?"

"Yes, Sister. It's so hot."

"Offer it up."

"Excuse me?

It might have been September, but it was still ninety-five degrees out and with the humidity probably a hundred and fifty inside. We were dressed in wool skirts and blazers. With her folded white handkerchief, she illustrated her martyrdom, daintily mopping shiny droplets of sweat on her mustachioed upper lip. And no wonder, shrouded as she was in two tons of gabardine. But did that mean we all had to suffer?

"Take it down. That *ponytail*. This isn't prom night." Imperious, she swirled toward the blackboard. Then back again. Her arm still poised in midair, a stick of chalk raised like a baton, "And Miss Doherty, that skirt of yours, which you have rolled up—you really thought I wouldn't notice?—had better be covering your knees. In fact, come kneel on the floor and let me see if touches the floor. If not, you will be kneeling on stones for an hour. Take notice, girls. Do you think this is the way our Blessed Mother would dress for school?"

At lunch, as we scarfed down Sky Bars and chocolate milk, Carrie reminded me, "Only one more year, we're out of here. Then it's college and *freedom*."

I hardly cared. My knees hurt like hell.

* * *

When I was fourteen, during a theatre workshop for high school students at Emerson College, I discovered that I wanted to be an actress. I wasn't exactly a theatrical novice. My mother had started me at Kay McDermott's Dancing School at two and a half, and I had performed solo in song and dance routines until I was twelve. But this was different. I played Ismene in a scene from Anouilh's *Antigone* with a girl from Milton Academy. She was my first WASP. She was already sixteen and wore a French twist and black turtlenecks to hide the hickies, she said, and claimed to have cocktails with her parents. She took me to buy blue jeans at Walkers, a Western store on Tremont Street. My mother made me return them.

"No daughter of mine will be seen wearing dungarees," she said. Mum was known for her pinky-beige wardrobe.

But my true love that summer was Miss Cate, the drama teacher, even though, after class, she was the Borden's Milk Lady, Miss Bessie, handing out ice cream samples on Boston Common. She wore a milkmaid's costume and stood holding the reins of a real cow.

"Have to pay the rent," Miss Cate would sigh.

I knew, with her deep, rich, silky voice, her grace and loveliness, and especially her unexpected kindness toward me, that she was a *real* actress. I wanted to be just like her. My dream for college was to be accepted into the drama department at Carnegie Mellon. Miss Cate went to Carnegie Mellon.

* * *

I went for my required college guidance meeting with Stigmata the fall of my senior year.

"So just where are we applying, Miss Doherty?"

I hated telling her my plans. "Carnegie Mellon, Sistah."

"No, no, no," she said with a smirk, "Carnegie Mellon is not appropriate." She glanced at the papers on her desk that she had asked me to fill out.

"Why not?" I blurted.

"'Why not, *Sister Stigmata*?' I won't tolerate any sassiness from you, young lady."

"I'm sorry, Sister. . . Stigmata."

"Carnegie Mellon," she continued, "is in a bad section of Pittsburgh and not a safe place for a young lady. No, I will not write a recommendation for you to go there. And without my recommendation, you can't go anywhere."

"But I want to be an actress!"

"Ahh, I see. Well, there are plenty of Catholic colleges you can apply to for theatre arts . . . You know, I was quite the actress, myself."

I bet. This woman was nothing if not dramatic.

"Not professionally, of course."

She smiled like she was sharing some private joke with herself. "It could happen to you, Miss Doherty." She sighed wistfully, shuffling and straightening the papers on her desk. "It's often girls like you, girls with worldly ambition, who get The Call."

"The call? You mean to be a star?"

She snapped back with a verbal shiver, "Of course not! *THE* Call! To be a nun!"

Disgusted, she reached for a sip of water. Then she fixed me with her beady eyes. Her gaze narrowed and darkened, she licked her colorless lips, and with a sly, sinister smile she said, "Mark my words, Miss Doherty, it could very well happen, even to you."

* * *

Johnny had been working at Howard Johnson's all summer and continued some nights and Saturdays once school started up again. He spent all his money on cars, old wrecks for fifty, sometimes a hundred dollars. It didn't matter what they looked like as long as they ran. He had to replace them, usually every month—they only lasted that long.

In the privacy of those cars, things really heated up. We graduated to big fat orgasms, touching under clothes, moving against each other, in the comfort of those spacious seats.

"Ya know I've never seen . . . ya know . . . a boy before." It was so . . . exotic.

"Well, I've never seen a girl before, either," Johnny said expectantly.

"Oh."

I hesitated. My Bermuda shorts were already unzipped, but . . . "All right." Holding my breath, I hooked my thumbs under the band of my shorts and the elastic of my underpants and scooched them down to my thighs.

The cops patrolled the parking lot frequently, flashing lights and knocking on steamy windows. I did not want to be caught like this. But I also wanted to make sure there was no way I was going to be caught getting The Call, either. I let Johnny have a good look.

He had this stupid grin on his face.

"You done?" I asked.

"Well, umm," he said, swallowing hard . . .

There was no chance I was going to be a nun.

Extra-Virgin

It was pouring. Inside, the bus already smelled like wet wool and B.O.

"Maybe it won't be so bad," said Carrie.

"Yeah, right," I answered.

The senior class trip: an eleven-hour bus ride to Canada, for ninety girls and three nuns, to Saint Anne de Beaupre, the Lourdes of Montreal.

"All right, girls," Stigmata announced, her black oxfords firmly planted as she straddled the aisle. "We'll begin our trip with a rosary. Take out your beads."

"Oh jeez, yeah, this is already the pits. Maybe we should pray for a miracle," I whispered to Carrie.

"Like what?"

"I don't know, something, anything. This is so perverted. The publics get to go to New York City or Fort Lauderdale."

"Can you imagine Stiggy in a two-piece?" Carrie could always make me laugh. At least we got to sit together.

"I think she shaves," I said, nudging Carrie, who attempted to stifle a snort. "No, really," I continued, "sometimes I see whiskers, sometimes not."

"The first sorrowful mystery," Stigmata intoned, trying to project over the sound of the bus's engine as it geared up for take-off, "The Agony in the Garden."

The bus coughed and lurched forward. Stigmata flew backward into the lap of Joan Donnelly.

"Sissssstttterrrrr!" Joan's shriek was audible but smothered under the weight of Stigmata's crushing monster-butt.

Carrie and I bent over to keep from detonating, smothering our guffaws in our skirts.

Carrie peered through her bangs, "Does that count as a miracle?"

* * *

For the next three days, we tracked down every church, shrine, and remote grotto in the vicinity of Montreal. At night, Carrie and I pooled together our stashes of candy and pigged-out, trying to erase the grease and disappointment of a monotonous diet of meatloaf and devotion.

On the fourth day, we arrived at the grand ecclesiastic finale, Saint Anne de Beaupre. I didn't bother to get out of the bus.

"I'm done."

"You're going to get in trouble," Joan Donnelly, always the priss, said as she passed. She was actually overheard to say at prom when her date tried to kiss her, "No, don't. I'm an Ursuline girl!" Stigmata's fave. And she had to be our roommate on this trip. Barf. At the last minute, Stigmata pulled a fast one and had dumped her in with us. Probably to spy.

"Well, Joan, I won't get in trouble, if you don't tell."

"Please," Carrie begged, "Come in with me. Besides, I have to pee."

"No. I refuse."

"Maybe there's a gift shop," she said enticingly, shaking a box of nearly empty candy Dots. "We're running low."

* * *

I was in the gift shop, deciding whether to do the Rolos or the Milky Ways, when Carrie rushed in.

"You've got to see this!"

We stood in a dark room whose walls were covered with discarded crutches and braces. On a stand, surrounded by votive candles, was a saint's severed, preserved hand on display in a glass case.

"Isn't it cool?" Carrie said, lighting a votive and kneeling, her hands clasped in prayer.

"Grisly . . . Carrie, you don't actually believe in miracles, do you?"

"Hey, if the lame can walk. Don't you?"

"I don't know. Maybe if I ever felt like God was actually around."

Stigmata popped her snarky old head into the shadows and pointed to her watch.

"Miss Doherty, time!"

"Witch," I whispered to myself, and then to Carrie, "I don't believe it, postcards?"

"C'mon! They're cool! I'm gonna send one to my cousin with the message: 'Here's a handy little item just for you!'"

After stocking up on more sweets, I met up with Carrie at the front of the church. She was cracking herself up as she dipped the tips of her fingers into the holy water font.

"What's so funny?"

"Look," she said.

I glanced behind her.

Brightly colored candy Dots decorated the large white plaster statue of the Virgin.

"Ha! Omigod, Carrie, you're wicked retarded!"

"Girls!" It was Stigmata, rounding the corner.

A green Dot, on the statue's modestly sculpted left breast, like a protruding nipple, slipped off.

Carrie pushed me out the door, "Run!"

* * *

For our last night in Canada, Stigmata announced that we were allowed to have a party in the gloomy, musty dining room of our small drab hotel. I was excited if for no other reason than to celebrate THE END. And we were finally allowed to change out of our uniforms.

"Are you coming?" Carrie asked, knocking on the bathroom door of the room we shared.

"You go. I'll be down in a minute." I was having trouble gluing on my first try at false eyelashes.

"What are you doing?"

"It's a surprise."

I had been studying the models in *Seventeen* and dreaming of Carnaby Street, and if this was my only opportunity for fun, then I was gonna dress for it. I couldn't wait to put on my first mini. In Filene's Basement, I had found a shiny green, black, and white zigzag print dress that I shortened to new heights. And, a la Twiggy, I wore large green ball earrings. Now, if I could only get this eyelash to stick.

I felt great, taking the opportunity to check out myself one more time in the hallway mirror outside the dining room.

"Gee," I thought, as I entered the party, "shouldn't there be music?" But what greeted me was a room full of pastel shirtwaist dresses, circle pins, and cardigans. And laughter. A swirling, hostile sea of laughter at *me*. Even the nuns snickered.

This can't be happening. Where's Carrie?

Across the room, Carrie had a bottle of Coke raised halfway to her mouth. Shock registered, passed, and then she grinned and nodded. My hand flew up, a measly brief wave, and feeling all of my five feet, ten inches, and fighting back tears, I sucked it up and joined her.

"Wow!" she said. "You look super good."

"I can't believe this." I slouched, my back to the room, my arms folded.

"They're just jealous," Carrie offered.

"Oh yeah, *right.*"

I curled up in my narrow bed that night, waiting for sleep and the dawn that would signal the end of this week in hell. What was wrong with me? Whatever possessed me to wear—as Stigmata proclaimed—that *immodest* get-up? Was I truly mental? Joan was already asleep and wheezing. Carrie tossed. I punched the pillow one more time and tried to will myself to sleep.

Intruding on the edges of my drifting consciousness, muffled sounds, like whispers. Figures, ghostlike shadows . . . And what? *WHAT??!!*

Water, cold and icy, flooded over me. Another gush. Water hitting me, harsh, like needles. Laughter. And a wail that was mine. More laughter, loud now. Footsteps running. The door slammed.

Carrie turned on the light, "Oh, God, are you all right?"

I sat up, stunned, drenched, and shaking. "No, I'm not all right! Fuck!"

"It was Louise and Megan," Joan called out.

"Assholes!" I jumped up and out of the wet bed. "Shit, god-dammit!"

"Stop swearing!" warned Joan.

"For God's sake, Joan, look at me! I'm soaked!"

I tore off my long wet orange nylon nightgown, emblazoned on the front with a big purple star, and threw it at her across the room. "Did you know about this?"

Joan shrieked, staring, "Oh my God! Breasts!"

"What's the matter with you?" I yelled.

Joan cowered, her hands flying, crossing chastely over her flat flannelled chest, "I've never seen any before."

"No," I said, "but really—"

"I haven't, not for reals," Joan whimpered. She unfolded a stringy, crumpled tissue, looking for a dry spot. As she blew into it, I looked over at Carrie to check for her reaction, *Can you, like, believe this?* But then Joan said, wiping her nose, "Carrie knew."

"Whadda ya mean?" I felt the chill then, someplace deep, on the inside.

"I'm sorry," Carrie said, trying to avoid my gaze. She sat on the edge of her bed, her knee bent, picking at her toes. "I didn't know you'd get so mad."

"Carrie?" I whispered.

She screwed up her face, dropped the look, then got up and swiftly walked past me to my bed and started pulling off the wet blankets and sheets. "You can sleep in my bed," she said.

"You knew? Why, Carrie? Why would you do this to me?"

"I don't know. I'm sorry, okay?"

* * *

I spent the following week at home, sick in bed with a cold. I hurt all over.

* * *

Johnny took out a Camel, lit it, and let me have a drag.

"God, your fingers are stained yellow. You smoke too much," I said, hoping to change the subject.

I was leaving for college in two days, and even though he had been my boyfriend for three years and had just handed me the large size bottle of Arpege, I was still not gonna "do it."

He stared out the window, blowing smoke rings.

"Don't be like this. I just can't," I said.

"We're not gonna see each other till Thanksgiving."

"My point exactly." The only girls I knew who did "do it"— okay, only one, for sure, Candy Covello—got pregnant and disappeared from school, and the neighborhood. I was not going to end up like that.

* * *

Early the next morning, Johnny, dressed only in his boxers and still sleepy, let me into his apartment through the back door. His mother had already left for work and his father wasn't home yet from working the graveyard shift. We had an hour, Johnny said.

I followed him into his bed. We had never been together like this. But I still wasn't going to "go all the way." His breath was sour, but I tried not to care because officially this was our last time together. We both felt it. Soon we were naked and holding each other.

"I'm really going to miss you," he said.

I knew he would. Although unspoken, the intimacy between us provided true warmth and affection. I was deserting him.

"Okay," I said. "Let's, ya know."

"Really?" he asked, "Are you sure?"

"No," I answered. "But . . . yeah, okay."

I reached for him . . .

A key, turning in the lock!

"Oh, shit! My father!"

"What do I do?" But I was already up and throwing on my clothes.

The back door caught on the chain guard that Johnny had smartly fastened.

"John!" his father called out.

"Front door, front door," Johnny said to me, pulling up his shorts. "Okay, Dad!"

"Johnny!" I said, turning back once before I left him.

"Yeah?"

"I'm sorry."

He smiled, shrugged. We both knew it was goodbye.

Summer of Love/Fall Into Temptation

"Sister Stigmata's probably correct," Dad had said when I told him about her Carnegie Mellon embargo. College and my acting aspirations were cute to him but not important. "Better still, you should go to business school and learn to type."

Mum, with debutante-ball dreams of fluffy white gowns and deep curtsies, wanted me to attend Vassar. She was encouraged by our neighbor, then head of the Vassar alumnae association, who urged me to accept. But there was no way I was going to spend four more years at another all-girls school. I wanted boys at least as much as I wanted theatre.

It had only been a few months since Dad had allowed me to actually date. For years I had cried to my mother, "He's ruining my life!"

"He's afraid you'll get in trouble."

"What do you mean?"

"Now, Susan, I know the nuns probably taught you every-thing you need to know about the birds and the bees."

As *if*.

"But if you have any questions to ask me . . ." *Sure, Mum. Like that's gonna happen.* She still couldn't say the word *pregnant*, substituting *expecting* instead.

So I chose the Jesuit university Marquette, in Milwaukee, where Skip had gone. It was farther away than Dad liked, but it did fit Stiggy's dogmatic conditions, and Mum quickly tallied the gowns she had in her closet that would be available to me for fraternity dinner dances. I was assured from the catalogue that there was a drama department, and, given the exhibition of gorgeous guys from Sigma Phi Epsilon who filled our house during Skip's college vacations, there was the promise of ample testosterone at Marquette as well.

College life was about to explode in 1968. Students who began the year clean-cut and polished were, by spring, bra-less, wearing love beads, and sporting Afros. I arrived in a blue wool suit and stacked alligator heels, but by the end of Welcome Week, I was passed my first joint at a concert—one twang of the sitar and I was *gone*. I wrote Johnny a real "Dear John" letter. I auditioned for *Antigone* not feeling ready to take on the lead but winning it. I wore my zig-zag mini-dress in a contemporary production. Fuck you, Stigmata.

It was thrilling, all of it, but I still didn't feel like I fit. I had one friend, Shelton, a boy from the drama department. Late at night, we sat by Lake Michigan while he read aloud his anguished poetry. But he depressed me. So on Sunday afternoons, Skip, still in Milwaukee and tending bar, let me play the juke box and served me Salty Dogs: grapefruit juice and vodka.

Although Marquette was a big Greek school, I shied away from joining any group. Still bruised from my years at Ursuline,

I was not a sorority girl. But the legacy of brotherhood Skipper had secured during his years at MU brought his sister to the attention of the boys of Sigma Phi. Especially to Patrick Brown, the fraternity president.

Patrick happened to pass by while I sat alone in the student union on the day I received Johnny's angry response. In my breakup letter to him, I expressed my yearning: I wanted more out of life—there just had to be more—and I didn't think it was in Boston. He lashed back, called me a social climber. I was crushed. *A social climber?* That wasn't what I meant at all. I wasn't sure what this indefinable something *more* was, but I longed to find it.

"Hey, Boston-babe, why so sad?"

Patrick slid into the booth, snatched Johnny's letter out of my hands.

"Hey," I winced, feigning annoyance, and tried to grab it back, though I felt amazed and giddy with the attention. Not only was he a senior and wicked handsome, but his self-confidence and charged energy were magnetic. And he was talking *to me*!

He read a few sentences, got the drift, said, "Ya know what I want to do with this?"

"Nope."

"Tear it up and toss it in the trash. Cause that's where it belongs. This is garbage."

He crossed the few steps to the trash can, crushed Johnny's letter into a ball, and shot it in like he was making a basket.

Then he aimed all that great-looking, bold assurance at me, and scored.

* * *

On a Sunday afternoon, Patrick picked me up at my dorm. We tried to walk around the lake, but my nose hairs froze in the January cold. Besides, there was no way we could escape the stench of yeast from the breweries.

Back at his house, Patrick's roommates were engaged in their usual Sunday sprawl in front of the TV, keeping tabs on Green Bay. Murph was groping another of his revolving coeds, and Dan cuddled with Nancy, his fiancée. Jimmy, as usual, was alone and working on his second six-pack, the empties lined up against the wall on the back of the sofa.

"We're gonna take a nap," Patrick announced with a wink. "Try and warm up."

"Yeah, I bet," Jimmy said. He gave me yet another quick once-over, his eyes lingering on my breasts. Gave me the creeps.

I smiled at Nancy, hoped for some sign of reassurance. She was, after all, a senior and nearly married. She and Dan, Patrick told me, had been doing it for years.

* * *

Earlier that semester I had discovered I needed a parent's written permission for birth control pills. A girlfriend of another of Patrick's frat brothers had slipped me a note with the doctor's name. It seemed like all the couples went all the way. They seemed so grown-up and sophisticated to me, twenty-year-olds in sport coats and cocktail dresses.

I had phoned my mother. "Mum, I need a letter for the doctor so in case I get sick and need a prescription for, like, penicillin or anything, he'll have your permission on file."

"Of course," she said. "No problem." Mum loved and trusted doctors. She always dressed up for an appointment, and then it was dinner out to discuss the details of what the doctor did or did not find. She anticipated hospital stays, kept a bag packed with a new nightie and a pretty bed jacket, just in case.

"This does not say particularly for birth control." The doctor was annoyed. We both knew I was pulling a fast one.

"I know," I answered, but I looked him straight in the eye and didn't falter. He was not my mother's kind of doctor: no posh Beacon Hill address; no smiling receptionist; no Ivy-League-trained, silver-haired gentleman listening patiently to her complaints. I felt mortified as I perched in the cramped shabby office, at the top of the stairs of the slutty building, with the strange, dour man. He sighed, tossed the letter on the desk, and opened a drawer.

"Twenty dollars," he said, handing me a small white box that slid open to reveal a pile of pink pills.

* * *

We had had to wait for the pills to take effect, but the day had arrived. We lay on Patrick's single bed. We could hear the sounds of the roommates and the TV outside the door. The Packers were ahead 6-0.

Patrick had had sex with lots of girls, he said, but I thought our make-out sessions, in the three months we had been dating, seemed routine. I missed the long hours of exploration and excitement I had shared with Johnny. But that shouldn't matter, I told myself.

"It feels different together now that we're pinned, doesn't it?" he whispered.

This must be love, I assumed. For reasons which I could not fathom, he was in love with me. He thought I was smart and funny and liked to boast of my Boston pedigree, having grown up amidst the cornfields of Indiana. And I admired, respected him. We bonded over our mutual disgust and outrage at the war in Vietnam, attended peace rallies, signed petitions. He was hardly a radical, though. And, I admit, the intensity of SDS frightened me. But Patrick felt safe to me. Powerful and safe. He wanted to attend law school and then use his degree to help the poor and disenfranchised. He was doing what I knew I couldn't. It was important, I believed, to support *his* abilities. And I derived strength from the image of *us*, a unit. Together we embraced the heady crescendos of love and peace that were sweeping the campus, the country. I believed in him and our greater purpose as a couple. And being the Sweetheart of Sigma Phi couldn't help but assuage the lingering traces of Olive Oyl.

We snuggled under the blankets. The sheets weren't fresh, and I could smell the cigarette smoke from the living room. Patrick smiled down at me. He had a winning smile and smiled frequently. His father owned a dental lab, and Patrick was proud of the extensive and expensive work his father had done to his lower jaw following a football accident.

Touchdown for the Patriots. It was a tie game.

"I'm ready," said Patrick, his voice husky.

He pushed into me. At the contact, it hurt a bit, and I felt blood flow. In the next instant, however, I was transported, as if transcending the parameters of my known self. My awareness instantly submerged and expanded, uniting with the landscape and dark language encoded in my body. Yet it was not sexually arousing, nor climactic. The rapturous secrets were released from the source of something divine. And it was feminine: the power of the receptive. This is where woman reigns, I knew.

A cheer came from the living room. Green Bay had won the game.

We lay there, him spent, me lost in my experience.

"That was out of sight!" he exhaled.

He had no idea.

Pleased, he searched for my reaction, "Hey, where are you?"

"Patrick, I know what it means to be a woman!"

"Wow, babe, I'm so glad it was good for you," he said. "I love you."

"Yes," I whispered.

I couldn't wait to get out of there.

* * *

Back at the dorm, I was bursting with my new discovery. I tried to write about it but couldn't. I needed to *tell* someone! I ran up a flight of stairs, scoured the empty halls for someone to talk to. I found a small group of girls in Diane's room. Diane had wicked red lumpy acne but a warm smile, which was reflective of her, I hoped. I was so high one of the girls asked what I was smoking.

"Nothing. Listen, this thing happened to me."

I tried to describe the event using my new lexicon—*receptive, woman,* and *power*—but they looked at me like I was crazy and laughed. So I left and sat alone, curled up in the stairwell, hugged my knees, and tried to hold on to the feeling.

Marriage Blues, 1970s

During spring break of my sophomore year, Patrick and I were engaged. Although I was still a teen, my dad deemed me ready for marriage. And in my world, that's what you did. You grew up and got married. Or became a nun. And now we know that wasn't going to happen.

Dad made the right phone calls to his alma mater, securing Patrick's admittance to Boston College Law School. I transferred to Emerson, not majoring in acting but Theatre Education. More practical, Patrick urged. I lived at home, passing the days going to classes and planning the wedding with Mum. Patrick, who shared a roachy apartment in Cleveland Circle with a couple of other students, would stop by late at night for beer and sandwiches and a bit of nookie in the kitchen.

Sex never again transported me to a mystical state. Quite the contrary, with Patrick, it was always rote and obligatory. And as for my new understanding of "feminine consciousness," well, it was like I had been given some amazing but way-too-fancy gift for my everyday life. So I tucked it away, buried it deep, tried to fit in and be normal. Be accepted. Be loved.

* * *

On August 26, 1970, the Women's Strike for Equality was an international event, the rallying cry: Don't Iron While the Strike is Hot! I married Patrick on August 27. I was twenty years old. It was humid and sticky that morning as Dad escorted me out of the house and down the brick path, in my gloriously gorgeous princess drag, to the waiting stretch limo. Suddenly fear seized me, a deafening roar, tightening my chest. I gasped for air. "Daddy, wait," I croaked. My vision blurred, my perspective warped. The vehicle before me was a hearse, festooned with funereal blossoms. Helpless, I was being sucked under a rapid current which I could not fight.

"No!"

"What? What's the matter?" He gripped my elbow, tighter.

"I don't think I can do this." I stammered.

"What? Well, you *will* do this." He raised his meaty finger, pointing it in my face. "It's too late. Get in the car."

Carrie, my maid of honor, was seated inside, poised on the velvet banquette, swathed in peach silk. I flung myself beside her, grabbed her hand as Dad slammed the door shut behind me. Startled, she questioned, "Susan?"

"I don't think I should do this!"

"Oh, God." She released my hand, turned away, kept her gazed fixed out the window. Dad climbed in, facing us, settled his bulk, positioning. Intractable. A bulwark of grim.

Three hundred and fifty guests witnessed the 11:00 a.m. Mass at Saint Ignatius Church on the Boston College campus and, later, celebrated at the Sidney Hill Country Club. Boston's

Democratic politicians, including the Massachusetts Attorney General, tossed back champagne with longhaired boys who smoked weed on the fringes of the golf course and girl cousins who only danced with each other.

A catered party continued at home, late into the night. I wandered from room to room, vaguely smiling and nodding, looking for a place to land. I drifted to the back porch, overlooking the patio, where my parents danced, showing off for the boozy crowd, twirling and dipping, to a jazz combo. I could hear my aunts in the kitchen—mixed with their laughter, ice cubes clinked against glass, bangle bracelets slid down a wrist. They talked of other weddings and honeymoon disasters: an unexpected thunderstorm, a flat tire, a gassy groom. The tone then shifted.

Aunt May's lilting soprano, "But, of course, there was poor Maureen. Ripped apart, she was, down there."

"Terrible, it was." Auntie Marge whispered. "Stitched up to the life of her."

My cousin Peter, a Celtic giant, a longshoreman like his father, worked in the shipyards of Quincy; he married Maureen, a girl from Ireland and, the story goes, she hemorrhaged on their wedding night.

I ran into my cousin Paulie on the stairs.

"Where's my fucking husband?" I asked, laughing as he blanched, enjoying his shock.

"He . . . he's in the playroom," he stuttered.

* * *

I stood in the doorway of the converted garage where Patrick played pool and smoked cigars with his frat brothers.

"Hey, babe," he said.

"Hey."

71

"My shot," he said, almost apologetically, clutching the stogie between his teeth.

"No, of course, go on." I turned away.

"Don't come in!" my cousin Patsy shrieked, her ruby lipstick smeared on the big teeth of her extreme overbite. She blocked the door to my bedroom, her fists full of rice, while behind her, my cousin Boots slid grainy handfuls between the layers of silky trousseau lingerie packed in the suitcase on my bed.

"Go away!" Patsy whined.

"Be a doll and come unzip me," Aunt May beckoned, heading for the bathroom. The condensation from a Tom Collins dripped from her grip. I followed her in and helped remove her party dress stained with sweat, as she reached unsteadily under her slip to undo the garters from her stockings.

"Auntie May, stay still!"

"Oh, honey, I'm so hot."

"You want some talc?" I offered.

"That would be great, sweetie."

She struggled out of her girdle, releasing her bound tummy and an enormous sigh.

I sprinkled the powder, her back sticky. The talc covered the freckles, the doughy roll above her nylon slip a dusty confection.

"Thanks, lovey," she said, in an inebriated haze. "Think I'll just sit here awhile."

She swayed to the toilet, sitting in front of the open screened window, and reached for her drink on the vanity.

"Do you want me to get Uncle Fred?" I asked.

"No, no," she waved me off. "I'll be fine. But let me tell you, sweetie, if I had to do it all over again, I never would've done it. Got married. Had kids. None of it."

I found Skip, who had flown in from California for the wedding, hiding out alone in the living room. I had pleaded with him to come. He and Dad never got along. Mum said it was because Dad was jealous when he returned home from the war and everyone fawned over the first grandchild.

I had shimmied down under the blankets many nights while Dad's angry voice bellowed through the darkened house. Skip had come home late again. "And you've been drinking, too, haven't you?" Dad would yell. Skip could barely whisper yes before the slap would come, stinging us all.

In college, girls chased Skip down the street shouting, "Paul! Paul!" due to his resemblance to the cute Beatle. Now with his long hair and beard, his appearance led Aunt May to exclaim that morning, as he escorted my mother down the aisle, "Oh, my God! It's Jesus Christ!"

I joined Skip, exhaled into the white sofa, all the plastic coverings removed for the occasion.

"When will I see you again?" I asked. "It's been so long."

"Come to California, sis."

Yeah, right, I thought. *There will be no California for me.* And then it hit me: *What have I done?*

Patrick appeared, announcing that it was time to go.

I cried as we backed out of the driveway in his VW bug, reaching out to kiss Skip goodbye.

"Why are you crying?" Patrick asked.

"Skip will be gone when we get back. I miss him."

Which was true, but what I didn't add was that I was stifling the scream, *Skip, help! Save me!*

* * *

After two days at the Waldorf Astoria, in New York City, we went to Grossingers, in the Catskills, a honeymoon gift from a client of my dad's. I was miserable, sunburnt and seated at crowded tables, squeezed between Patrick and round, squishy women with their loud children, who gobbled overflowing platters of food. All the while, on stage, the spotlight shined on crass comics and their insults.

I phoned home daily, charges reversed, for updates on the post-nuptial festivities still raging. Edward filled me in: Aunt Dot had walked in on Skipper and one of my half-naked bridesmaids, and party diehards were crashed on the lawn. How I wished I was part of it.

* * *

When we returned, Patrick and I settled into a rent-controlled apartment that my father paid for near the law school. I spent the first ninety days of my marriage secretly and obsessively counting off the dwindling days that I could still get an annulment in the Catholic Church—a sanctioned, holy getting-out-of-it . . . But I loved Patrick! What was wrong with me?

One day, while Patrick was at Dad's law firm to set up a schedule, which he would not keep, to clerk afternoons after class, Carrie came to visit. After smoking a joint, we canvassed the kitchen cabinets for munchies.

"Spam!" Carrie shrieked. "He eats *Spam*?!"

"Oh my God, I know! And anchovies on his pizza!"

We collapsed on the floor, convulsed in laughter.

"Oh," said Carrie, "this will never work."

* * *

Six months later, the ecclesiastic cut-off day had come and gone, and I was still Mrs. Brown. I lay on our bed weeping. I couldn't say why, but I kept imaging a dark tunnel that I could not escape.

On the eve of my twenty-first birthday, I couldn't pull out of it. Patrick got scared and called my parents. They came, bundled me off in their car, and tucked me into one of the boy's twin beds in the back bedroom. I quietly pulled out tufts of aqua chenille while Patrick snored beside me.

The next morning, they were all cheery, made me pancakes, and insisted we go shopping. All I really needed, they said. That night there was a family birthday dinner planned, but when I walked into the restaurant, in my new suede hot pants and silk blouse, a cheer rang out, "Surprise!" A band struck up the Beatles' "In My Life," and all my friends were there ready to party. Patrick and my parents stood there beaming and, well, I just had to be happy.

* * *

With the spring came student strikes in Boston and police in riot gear. I marched down Beacon Street, shouted, "Peace now!" and stood amongst the other anti-war demonstrators on the Common while Abbie Hoffman pointed to the spire of the John Hancock Building and declared, "That's a goddam hypodermic needle!"

Patrick sprinkled albumin flakes and blood, pricked from his finger, into his urine to flunk his draft physical and did, punctuating the experience by vomiting on the draft sergeant's shoes, just to make sure.

And sometimes he went out drinking with the guys, he said, to the strip joints in the Combat Zone. Soon after, he had a blister, he called it, on his penis.

* * *

I graduated, cum laude, in June. The ceremony was held at the Music Hall for the mostly stoned graduates, who passed joints in their caps and gowns while waiting to line up. Rod Serling, from *The Twighlight Zone*, was the featured speaker and shook my hand before the family celebrated with lobster at Pier Four. Outside, a new green Karmann Ghia convertible, with tan leather interior, was waiting for me from my parents, the antenna tied with a big yellow bow. And I had a job, hired as the creative drama teacher and tour director at the Boston Children's Theatre for the following fall.

Prior to graduation, that spring, I had starred in a one-woman show, at the Charles Playhouse, called *French Grey*, a one-act play about Marie Antoinette, the hour before she was to be guillotined. It was pretty intense material, even for a more seasoned professional, and I surely didn't shine, but subsequently I was asked by the producers to join a summer theatre in New Hampshire, where Patrick could easily commute to on weekends.

"No way," he said.

So I didn't. Instead, he worked that summer in the Attorney General's office, a plum assignment gratis my dad. I would join him at his after-work office shmoozes. Another girl in a cocktail dress.

September, I went to work at the Children's Theatre, and Patrick began his third and final year in law school. I loved my job working with the kids. We partied with friends. Ate dinner with my parents at least twice a week. And it was confirmed that Patrick would indeed join Dad's law practice after passing the bar exam.

"But Patrick," I asked, "what about your plans to help people? What about legal aid?"

"Hey, it's all working out as it should," he said.

* * *

Until the morning I walked out his door, knowing I would not return.

Mea Culpa No Mora

The sun was bright, the car a solarium. I opened the window, breathed deeply, realized it was time for Mum to know, that she was entitled to have her own opinion of me. Everyone else did. I had to tell her why: why the men who had professed to love me so much had turned their backs on me. There was no hiding it now; it was official: I was truly a bad girl.

It had happened while she was in Florida for her winter sojourn. When she returned, tanned and bejeweled, we sat in her baby-blue Cadillac. It was spring, but there were still patches of soot-fringed snow crusted on the sidewalks.

"I just don't understand," she said, checking her lipstick in the rearview mirror. "Your father said we'd have to move if you got a divorce 'What will people think?' he said. I told him I'm not worried about other people. My only concern is for our daughter!"

Obviously Dad hadn't told her why he had disowned me. She thought it was just because I was separated from Patrick.

So I told her about that winter. I had left Patrick with little explanation for leaving except for a force bearing down on me to be free. Just for a while, I said, hoping to placate him. I stayed with two girlfriends from Emerson in a tiny one-bedroom apartment on Beacon Street, teaching at the Children's Theatre and performing at the Loeb, in Cambridge. During this time, Patrick began following me. Off and on he would turn up, sitting in his car, watching. One night, the roommates away, he burst into the apartment while I was in bed with Drew, our mutual friend.

We had known Drew from the first week that Patrick started law school. He was one of a group of us who bonded over politics and music. He was the coolest, brilliant and lazy, a spoiled rich kid from Manhattan whose smirk flagrantly displayed his disdain for the other straighter students. He was getting his law degree for his parents, he claimed. He really wanted to be a writer.

What I didn't tell my mother was that Drew had given me Quaaludes and taken me to see *A Clockwork Orange*, that I had been overcome by the grotesque images in the film. Or that when we returned from the movie and were alone, he had knocked the cigarette out of my hand and proceeded to kiss me. Falling onto the waterbed, we had sex, but I was so drugged, I soon passed out. Until suddenly there was shouting and lights and Patrick, his face contorted, so hateful, above me. He grabbed my hair, yanked me out of the bed, and threw me onto the floor. I crawled, tried to reach for a nightgown on the chair. He snatched it away, hissed, "Oh, no, you don't! Is this one I gave you?"

Drew scrambled to get dressed. "Oh, man, sorry. Shit, Patrick. Let's talk." Patrick just laughed, repelled, and stormed out. Drew followed him. All I could do was remain on the floor and weep.

Soon rushed footsteps padded down the hall. I looked up, tried to focus through my haze. Standing over me were the two guys from the apartment downstairs, Paul and Vincent, scrawny, pale and panicked, holding hands in their white underpants. They looked so sweet and scared and funny that I had to laugh before lapsing back into tears.

"What happened, honey? Oh my God! Are you all right?"

They wrapped me in a blanket and settled me on the couch. Paul ran down to his apartment, returned with a Valium that he urged me to take.

At dawn, I awakened, alone and frightened. My body was bruised and the crown of my head smarting—my fingers gingerly traced a nickel-size bald spot. The intensity of the terror and sadness became overwhelming. I called my doctor's service, thinking to leave a message, but the operator put me right through to him.

"What's going on?" he said.

"I didn't think I'd get you."

"I was in town last night. It was too late to go home, so I slept at the office."

I told him what happened. To my surprise, he said, "I'll be right over." It was barely light out.

Dr. Blake had been my gynecologist for two years. He was young, kind, and always caring. I trusted him. We had gone through birth control talks and diaphragm fittings. Although I was surprised at his house call, I thought that, well, he must also be a friend.

When he arrived, we sat on the couch. He gave me another pill and put his arm around me, caressing my back, massaging my neck. And then he held me, kissed me, and whispered how he felt so much more for me than just being my doctor.

I pulled away, "No. I can't. Please, no." I wanted to shout, *What are you, crazy? What are you doing?* And maybe I did. I just remember that the room was still and spinning at the same time.

"I just want to make you feel better," he crooned, his hand

jamming into my jeans, my crotch, his fingers searching. "Relax, I know what you need. Trust me."

"Please stop. Don't!"

He sat back, removed his paws, threw his arms up, clasping them behind his head. "Come to my office later, I see special patients then." He winked, then tenderly added, "I have a vibrator. Sweetheart, I know what you need."

He jumped up, mumbling about breakfast and eggs and cholesterol. His hunger must've shifted. He was gone.

The phone rang. It was Patrick.

"You have until noon to get all your things out of this apartment, or I'll call your father and tell him what a slut you are. It's about time you're knocked off your pedestal."

By the time I tracked down some coffee and a friend with a car, ready to take me from downtown to Brighton, the weather was near blizzard conditions. I called Patrick "Please, couldn't this wait till the weather clears?"

"No, now, or I'll call your father."

What was normally a twenty-minute drive stretched into almost two hours as the car barely crawled through the snowy streets. The weather reflected how I felt: thick, congested, icy.

We arrived at quarter to twelve. Patrick opened the door, sneering.

"I just want you to know, I already called your father."

The hurt started low. I stumbled back, hit the wall behind me, and slid down. In the narrow hallway with the lingering odor of steamed cabbage and now my remorse, I began to wail. Broken.

* * *

Back in the apartment on Beacon Street that night, I called my father. "Daddy?"

"What do you want?"

"Daddy, I'm so sorry."

"Yeah? Well, you're not my daughter. I don't want to hear from you again."

"Daddy!"

The phone clicked dead.

I joined Paul and Vincent, who sat on the living room floor eating pizza, amidst the strewn artifacts and attire that I was able to collect earlier.

"What happened?" asked Vincent.

"Wow. I guess my father just disowned me."

I felt strangely peaceful, released from the crushing constraints of his love. And for the first time that day, the crying stopped.

* * *

"Mum?"

She had been silent for a long time.

"Do you want me to get out?"

"No, don't go," she said.

She stared straight ahead, through the windshield, as if seeing through to her own clarity.

Slowly, she began to erupt. "I am so angry!"

"Mummy, I'm really sorry."

"I'm not angry at you! Why do you think I go to Florida every year? If I didn't, I'd go mad! I went from a domineering mother to a domineering husband!" She was shaking, her fingers skittish, nervously tapping the steering wheel. "I am sick and tired of the double standard! Look, I don't condone what you did, but I understand it. You were vulnerable, you wanted comfort. You didn't deliberately set out to hurt Patrick or your father as they most certainly have done to you!"

"Mum?" I had never heard her talk like this. "Thanks, but I—"

"Susan, don't you understand? You are me."

California Kaleidescope

1972.

I was in California to establish residency for a divorce, which was my dad's demand relayed via my mother. He didn't want me getting a divorce in Massachusetts. "It's the least you can do," he said. He'd pay all expenses.

I might have been kicked out of the kingdom, but I was finally liberated. On my own and out of my dad's ruling realm. On the plane heading west, I felt as if I was being transported toward the warm, buttery light I had always imagined, yearned for. Yes! My life was about to commence.

I arrived looking the part of a flower child, in bell-bottoms and tie-dye, but my long hair had been tended to at Michel Kazan's Salon at the Ritz-Carlton, and my leather boots were from Bonwit Teller. I signed with a modeling agency in the city, and for the first few months I slept on the couch in Skip's living room in Mill Valley, where he lived with his pregnant "old lady."

I attempted hostessing at The Trident, but the management complained that I wasn't loose enough, too polite. I addressed the patrons with *yes, ma'ams* and *no, sirs*.

I waited tables one night, just cocktails, dropping two full trays of drinks.

* * *

Skip gave me Omar's number.

"Call this guy. He's solid."

Omar was different from Skip's other friends, the rock gods and the freaks. Omar was hip, yet he had it together in the business world. An entrepreneur, he owned restaurants and real estate. I moved into one of his houses in Marin, on Mt. Tamalpais, with his Dutch business partner, Nicholas, and Martin, Omar's "genius" chef.

Nicholas had a wife and son in Holland. One night when we were sharing a bottle of wine and discussing Nabokov, he said, "I wish tonight you were my lady."

"Ya, well, I'm not," I answered.

Another night, I awoke to Martin, his breath reeking with alcohol, sitting expectantly next to my bed.

"No way, Martin."

* * *

I was sitting in Omar's offices in Union Square. He had given me the name of a colleague at North Beach Leather who would lend me outfits for a photo shoot. Omar had this idea that I should do a publicity poster to announce my arrival on the West Coast. His vision posed me on a Harley, classy and elegant, a posse of gnarly bad-ass dudes in the background.

Omar liked advising me, which was appreciated, because although Skip had welcomed me with open arms, he wasn't exactly around much. He managed rock groups and had groupies from his own star-turn, involved in the creation of the Trident. The first night he enthusiastically picked me up at the San Francisco Airport, whisking me off to a Rolling Stones concert. But he was having trouble enough keeping his own life on track.

I hoped to be Omar's girlfriend, but then he told me he already had one. A flight attendant. Which hadn't prevented him from sleeping with me.

"I can't believe you have a girlfriend. I don't understand, I thought we—"

"She's gone a lot. Look, I think you're lonely and you should go home."

"I don't know what I am, and I can't go home."

He nodded, smiled, but looked impatient. Dismissive.

I was pissed. "Well, I'm not about to become the house whore. And I hate modeling!"

I left his offices, bought some flowers at the corner. It amazed me that I could buy flowers year-round at open markets. So unlike Boston.

Screw Omar, I thought, and screw him for saying I should go home, except as I made my way through the five o'clock commuters, on my way to catch the ferry back to Sausalito, I was overcome with loneliness.

* * *

I was definitely not fitting in. I had been in California for six months, and I was still having trouble getting the feel for a ripe avocado. And that wasn't all. I had tried to be hipper. I sunbathed topless and made out with pony-tailed musicians. I listened to

85

Joni Mitchell and said things like "groovy" and "far out." Smoked opium, downed MDA, and inhaled Tequila Sunrises. I had a cool, young black attorney from Petaluma handling my divorce. I danced all night at music-industry parties where long banquet tables held drugs, liquor, and whole roasted pigs.

And I was learning that "free love" meant loving everybody but being free enough to not particularly care about anyone. Which really meant it was just about fucking. Which left me feeling even more alone. Empty. A new and terrible kind of lonely.

* * *

A few weeks later, I had a date with Ron, a guy who did something in the music business, I wasn't quite sure what. He picked me up with his friend Joe, who worked for Sly Stone, and Joe's date. We went to dinner in the city and then to a party back in Marin. On my way to the bathroom, I met up with the drummer of a major band whose phone calls I had not returned.

"Hey, baby, what's up with you?"

"You're married," I answered.

"Yeah, so?"

"So don't call me!"

When I returned, Joe passed me a joint.

"This is some powerful shit, man." He nodded to make his point. "It's Thai."

Ron was being very sweet and he was definitely attentive, but I got the whirlies from the weed and felt more sick than sexy. Music was pounding while some rocker screeched, "This is my world!" drawing whoops and cheers from the crowd. All I could think was, "This is nowhere." I called a taxi.

The next morning I woke to the news that as the party neared dawn and a few stragglers remained, the drugs got heavier and some thugs on PCP beat up Ron and Joe and raped Joe's date.

That day, I sold my Beetle to Omar for a thousand dollars, packed up, and flew south.

* * *

After a stint with family friends in Westwood and lunches at the Polo Lounge, I moved in with two queens at the Casa del Mar apartments on Sunset Boulevard in West Hollywood. Nick was a guest makeup artist I met the year before at a cosmetics counter in Boston. We had clicked then, and now we were inseparable.

He cut my long blonde hair (time to lose that *Alice in Wonderland* look, he said) and dyed it red. He dressed me in vintage dresses from the flea market and platform shoes from Neiman's and insisted on calling me Nora, from *The Thin Man*. He took me to bars where I was always the only girl—the only real one.

* * *

"Happy Birthday, Nora!"

Nick and his clan were gathered in the dining room around the decorated ice-cream cake.

"Open your gift, darling!"

A black baby doll.

"Thanks, boys." Air kisses all around.

"Darling," Nick proclaimed. "You are so fabulous! I adore you!"

We shared a bed, cuddling at night. In the morning, we awakened, our fingers linked in easy innocence.

As our intimacy deepened, I wanted him to love me like a man. I was having trouble understanding that when a gay man said he adored you, he didn't mean *all* of you. It became odd, and then hurtful, to not be wanted because I was a woman. I was crazy about Nick, but no matter how fabulous he thought I was, I was not fabulous enough. So one night, to please me, he attempted, but not for long.

Work-wise, I made half-hearted attempts meeting with agents, never quite making it to all the interviews. After two months, I got a call to appear on a soap but was too tired to show up. Exhausted all the time, I became Nick's made-up doll, propped on our peach-satin-draped bed.

When I could barely lift my head off the pillow, I made the call I dreaded.

"Dad?" I pleaded, "I need to come home."

* * *

The family doctor said my divorce was the reason I felt poorly. He prescribed putting cracker crumbs in my mattress to help me get out of bed. I was back in Boston, back in the single-girl bed, in the room with the lavender wallpaper with blue butterflies and the white French-provincial furniture.

After the doctor's visit, I cried to Edward, "I'm really sick and no one believes me."

"I believe you, Ya-Ya," he said, reverting back to his childhood nickname for me, "but I don't know what to do."

A few days later, I sat at the kitchen table, my head in my hands. I looked up as my mother walked into the room.

"Oh my God!" she exclaimed, "You're orange!"

"You see it, too?"

"Yes, of course!"

I was so relieved. When I had caught my tinted reflection in the bathroom mirror that morning, I thought I was crazy.

Infectious hepatitis.

Being sick was hardly fun, but I was relieved to be diagnosed, relieved to be taken care of, relieved to have a time-out. All my playmates in L.A. had to get gammagobulin shots, which they were not happy about. However, seeing me frail and deathly did lead my dad to forgive me, did lead him to want to include me in the family again.

Yet the truth smarted: There was no relief, no prescription for what lay beneath my nausea and fatigue—the knowledge that I had had my chance out in the world and I had failed.

Wounded Hero

1973.

He was easy to spot. And not just his shaggy hair and beard, lacy shirt, and leather vest. It was the way he moved—freely, animated—darting among the reserved international sophisticates. I was on an upper deck of the *Michaelangelo* as it left New York harbor when I first spied him. He was on the deck below, sprinting from rail to rail, waving goodbye.

I was still in the hospital when Dad announced he was taking Mum and me to Europe. Great, Europe! But a *cruise*? *You mean like bingo and a lot of drunk middle-aged men in white shoes?* I wanted to hop on a plane and be there. But since I was still in recovery mode, I tried to get into it. *Okay, I'll read and reflect—yeah, that sounds good. And possibly try to figure out what to do with my life.*

It was early June and, despite being chilly, I was tempted by my reserved deck chair and a siesta in the sun. *Oh damn! What's he doing here?*

Shaggy-hair guy sat in cut-offs, cross-legged and bare-chested on a low square table that separated my lounge from another fellow in a Speedo, with slick black hair, tanning his already-bronze torso. I could turn back, but that meant being sequestered in the suite with my parents. Oh no, shaggy-hair guy looked up. He grinned at me briefly and then returned to his book. Well, he's seen me now, and it would be weird to turn away. I eased myself into the chair and closed my eyes, putting out a don't-mess-with-me vibe.

Just relax. God, he's so close, I can hear him breathing. And his jewelry! As he turned the pages of his book, his many bangle bracelets rang and clattered.

Speedo-guy chose that moment to erupt in an exasperated Continental accent, "You are not supposed to be sitting there! This is my table, and your jewelry, it's like bells, clang, clang! You are too noisy!"

"Um, excuse me," I intervened, "I assume, then, that this is my table, as well, and I'd like him to sit here." *What am I doing?*

Speedo-guy jumped up, summoning a white-jacketed attendant lurking nearby, all the while gesturing and shouting in Italian.

"Hey, that was cool," Shaggy-hair guy said, turning to me with a broad grin. "*You're* cool."

I smiled back. It was all pretty funny. "No problema, but he probably won't like us laughing at him."

"No, you're probably right," he said, closing his book, *Be Here Now.*

"Great book," I said.

"Yeah," he nodded, looking a bit surprised at my response.

He scooted off the table, breezily tossed me another grin and a wink.

"Hey, I'm Paco, see you around."

"Yes, okay, sure . . . and hey—I'm Susan."

"Ciao, sweet Sue."

He then greeted the attendant familiarly in Italian and clapped him on the back, Paco's continued amusement apparent as the two of them sauntered off together arm in arm.

*　*　*

I was ensconced in the first-class cabaret with Lola, from Manhattan, and chunky Louis, her diamond-merchant husband. Lola had already assumed the role of my shipboard social info-diva, filling me in on pedigrees and prospects. The roster included members of a social milieu who were apparently accustomed to traveling in the same circles.

"That table over there," she pointed out, "Agnellis. And those two gentlemen, cousins." She leaned in farther, her eyebrow arched. "From one of Mexico's wealthiest families."

"I don't care how rich they are." I retorted.

She arched her perfectly drawn, skeptical brow.

"No really, I don't, Lola, but the one on the left is incredibly . . ."

"Gorgeous," she interrupted. "Like an Aztec god."

"And I'm not immune to beauty. I can't take my eyes off him. Oh, no, he's getting up. This is embarrassing . . . he's coming over here!"

"See, a god. He heard my prayer," sighed Lola. "Sorry, Louis."

"Hello," he said, standing before me. "My name is Ismael. Would you care to dance?"

*　*　*

"You've got to be kidding! Is this the only song they know?"

A three-piece combo, tucked into a corner, was playing a punishing rendition of "Tie a Yellow Ribbon Round the Old Oak Tree."

Gathering me into his arms, Ismael crooned, "I know where we can go. Are you up for an adventure?"

Ismael took the lead down several flights of curving narrow metal stairs. We moved quickly through the labyrinth of steel passageways and empty corridors.

"You've done this before, right?" I asked. Where the hell was he taking me?

"Yes, yes, of course," he laughed. "You'll like it very much."

We continued on, pausing only to stand hushed and awed as we glimpsed through a porthole: a naked woman astride a young man on the floor, his officer's uniform lying crumpled in the shadows beside them.

I tugged at Ismael's sleeve as we slipped away. "Was that it?" I whispered.

"No, no," he laughed.

As we reached what was surely the bowels of the ship, Ismael pushed through a set of double doors, swiveling to catch my reaction.

I gasped at the sight before me—the tourist-class disco—the rock band loud, the crowd wild. Ismael led me into the mass of gyrating bodies until the heat and sound and faces became a throbbing blur and we had to burst out into the chill of the night air.

It was well past four when we found our way back up to the tamer regions of first class, where we joined a group tranquilly settled out under the ink-stained night and a catalog of glittering stars.

Ismael draped a plaid wool blanket around my shoulders and, while sipping cognac from his silver flask, entertained the others with details of our adventure, including the sexual exploits of the indiscriminate couple.

"Now, I think it is time for bed." He stood, stretching. I was dazzled.

He offered me his hand, "Are you coming?"

Hmm, so very tempting. "Ah, no," I sighed, "not this time."

He shrugged, keeping my hand to kiss. "Goodnight, then."

I watched him as he strolled away humming, his fingers lightly trailing the railing . . . gorgeous. Couples drifted off, whispering, giggling. I closed my eyes, grateful for the luxurious absorption of the stillness.

"Hey you, isn't it past your bedtime?"

Like a weary sailor's apparition, shaggy-hair guy was approaching.

"Paco?" His sudden appearance gave me a start. "You scared me!"

"Didn't mean to do that," he replied, crouching down next to me.

"Strange, but I didn't hear you coming," I said, referring to his infamous clanging jewelry.

"Yeah, well," he laughed, "you were distracted."

He took out a pouch of Drum tobacco and rolling papers from his vest pocket.

"Mmm," I watched him roll the shag. "Smells good."

"So, what do you know about Ram Dass?" He handed me a cigarette.

The tobacco was strong and burny. "Not much," I coughed.

"Easy, girl."

"But the book was like, wow! I loved it." I was feeling kind of lightheaded. "What's in this stuff?"

"Just tobacco. 'Like, wow'?" he teased.

"Well, I . . . I don't know how to explain it."

"Give it a try. I'm not going anywhere."

"Hmm, yeah," I sighed, relaxed and oddly comfortable with this curious man. "Okay, some years ago I had this amazing experience, like . . . like slipping into another dimesion."

"Stoned?"

"Unh-unh." I shook my head, drawing on the ciggie.

"Tripping?"

"Nope. Sometimes I think I must've dreamed it. Yet it was more real than anything I've ever known."

"Like seeing behind the veil?" he offered.

"Yeah, something like that. So when I read *Be Here Now*, I thought, wow, Ram Dass would understand. Someone would understand."

"Cool."

We continued to chat some; however, it was the comfort of a sublime ease in the silence which drew me closer into his companionship. Leaning into the other, our shoulders bounced back and forth, playful and familiar. At dawn we followed the awakening, a sizzling palette of psychedelic pomegranate and mango. A bright golden blade shot out, finding us, stabbing me with light.

"Okay, that was a *wow*, right?"

"Of course, Miss Susannah." His expression was still amused; his eyes were kind.

"I'd better go in." I sighed, sleepy and content.

"Yeah, but let's do this again. Have another smoke. Ciao, bella."

When I entered my stateroom, my father was up and pacing.

"Where have you been?" he demanded.

"What do you mean, Dad? On the ship. Watching the sunrise."

His face was scarlet and pinched with fury. He hadn't hit me, not in a long time, but still, I froze.

"Daddy, where could I go?"

* * *

He stayed in bed, all that day and into the night, his face to the wall.

My mother joined me for dinner. "He made himself sick, waiting up for you all night. 'Xavier,' I told him, 'she's fine.'"

96

"Mum, look, I'll probably be out again all night tonight, so if he's going to do this for the whole trip, I'm going to take the first plane back home when we dock."

She looked nervous—afraid of Dad as we all were, undoubtedly more—but she agreed to relay my message.

* * *

Each night thereafter, sometimes after I left Ismael's stateroom, Paco would find me, and we'd sit out under a constellation-embroidered sky. Starved, I was suddenly feasting, filling up the space inside myself that consumed words like *truth* and *goodness*, *compassion* and *spirit*. I craved just the sound of his voice.

Toward dawn, groggy but becalmed, we'd observe the lights, shining from the portholes, dim on the blue-black sea, bobbing like scattered, unstrung pearls.

* * *

"Are you awake, sweetie?"

It was Lola. I was stretched out under the sun trying to make up for lost hours of sleep.

"Barely," I answered. "What's up?"

She perched on the edge of the deck table.

"Well, hon, you do know who your boyfriend is, don't you?"

"Ismael? Yes, Lola, you filled me in."

"No, doll, the other one . . . Frank Serpico."

"You mean Paco?" I laughed. "He's not Frank Serpico."

I tried to recall the article and the picture of the New York cop I had seen months earlier in a magazine.

"Yes, he is. Everyone knows."

I grabbed my sarong and went in search of Paco. I was upset, felt oddly betrayed.

When I found him, he was walking Alfie, his Old English sheepdog. I fell in beside him.

"Hey, look who's here, Alf."

I got right to the point.

"Paco, are you Frank Serpico?"

He glanced away, then back. His look was hard, "No."

Then he smiled, and in that smile I read: *Yes, I am, but please, not between us.*

"Okay, Paco." I linked my arm through his.

* * *

"He's a nut," said Dad, pouring himself another goblet of wine.

"Daddy, he's not. He cares about things."

"I think they're making a movie about him," chirped Mum.

"Yeah, yeah, big deal," Dad responded. "He's still a nut."

I wasn't going to let him get to me. I was in Rome, and I was with Paco, and it was our last night together.

Paco picked me up at the hotel in the orange VW camper that he had transported over on the ship. We drove to a café for espressos. Fueled, we walked for hours, our bodies molded, pressed into each other. Inscrutable shuttered windows lined ancient streets, the atmosphere thick with other lovers' stories. Each step bound us closer, drawing us together toward a tomorrow.

Later, back in the van, we waited again for the sunrise. Paco was leaving that morning to drive to Switzerland and I, to Greece, to Corfu, to the hotel of family friends. But the shift between us was palpable.

"Come with me," he said.

"I can't, not now."

I wanted to be with him, and I knew that I would, but I also knew that I wasn't strong enough then—not in body, not in spirit—to be the kind of woman I wanted to be for him. And besides, I couldn't do that to my parents. This trip was a big deal. It had taken a long time for me to finally realize that my dad showed his love by providing for his family.

"I will, though, I promise."

He handed me a slim paperback.

"T.S. Eliot . . . a favorite?"

"Yeah, *The Lovesong of J. Alfred Prufrock.*"

I opened the book and read the inscription: "To Susan, whose scars I love. Be happy, you. —Paco."

Lusting For It

....

1974.

The winter following our return from Europe, I leased a studio apartment in an old ivy-covered brick building in Cambridge, a short walk to Harvard Square, living alone for the first time, at twenty-four. The rooms had sunny windows and crown molding, and there was a fireplace. I finally got to unpack: a print of Botticelli's **Venus** from the Uffizi Gallery, a flea-market bust of the goddess Diana, a flokati rug from Greece. I set up my little piece of girl-heaven.

I taught part-time, performed at the Loeb, and hung out with Carrie and friends from Marquette who also lived nearby. Most of the time, however, I was content to be pulled in and reading: Hesse, Anaïs Nin, Isadora Duncan—and *Serpico*, learning more about the cop who made headlines, the man I felt compelled to be with. Our time together, though mercurial, was potent and suspended from our personal story lines. Now the account of his saga—his brave lone voice against corruption and graft within the police force and the brutal consequences, being ostracized and shot—impacted me. I admired his courage, his moral outrage, his goodness, and I longed to imitate it. My plan was to reunite with him—strong, and worthy of the relationship I wanted. The one he deserved.

By spring, I found a way to return to Europe—which really meant a return to Paco. I was accepted to an actors' training program at the Royal Academy of Dramatic Art, in London. It was important to me to have a purpose aside from what I was ready and willing to explore with him. The promise of RADA gave me that.

I sent Paco a note about my plans to travel to England but told him that I would first go to Switzerland and find him. I don't know why I didn't tell him exactly when I would arrive, except perhaps to maintain some sense of independence, or, more likely, to stave off the possibility of his rejection. I needed to keep the dream alive right up to the last.

Throughout the year we had exchanged letters—short lyrical messages, really—and there was a brief transatlantic call that he surprised me with, full of heightened inflection but very little content.

I departed from Logan Airport amidst a giddy farewell from my girlfriends and parents. I was more excited than nervous as I folded into the soaring wings of Swiss Air—until I was gripped by the enormity of the journey before me and the romantic stakes I had created for myself.

I got off the train from Zurich in Montreux with my large black canvas bag hanging off one shoulder and a soft leather valise tucked under the other. Bleary-eyed, I crossed to the hotel. After checking into a room with French doors that opened to a view overlooking the lake, I wrote on hotel stationery, "Paco, I am here," drawing a loopy arrow up to the hotel's signature embossment. I carried the sealed envelope next door to the post office where I knew he drove weekly from the Alpine village of Leysin to pick up his mail. Back in my room, I climbed under the quilt and crashed.

The next morning, the heavy gray mist that covered the lake also enveloped me as well. The bleakness consumed me: What if he doesn't come? What if he does?

Neither the daylight that eventually broke through nor the snowcapped vistas nor the loveliness of the swans, partnered forever, gliding along the sweep of lakeside before me, could get me out of that room.

I waited. Day turned into night turned into day and night again.

On the third day, I had to leave the hotel for cigarettes. Just as I came out of the hotel and stepped out onto the sidewalk, Paco's orange van pulled into the street. Instant joy! It was him—the dark shaggy hair, the black shirt. Then, panic! On the passenger seat beside him: a blur of long blonde hair. I turned, ran into the hotel, through the lobby, to a back exit that led down to the lake. I walked, sometimes ran, ranting, "You bloody idiot! Of course he has a woman! You stupid fucking idiot!"

An hour later, as I ducked across the lobby, the concierge called out, "Miss Doherty! You have a message!"

I grabbed it, mumbled thanks, and slipped back into my room. My heart thumping, I read: Susan! Got your note, but you aren't here. I'll check back later. —Paco."

Okay, so I have to do this. I'll just say hello, meet the woman, then off to London. I had unpacked very little making it easier to pull together for my escape. I changed, though, into my favorite pink Indian cotton halter mini-dress—needed to look really great. Then I sat on the bed before the phone, my heart clenched, and waited for the ring.

* * *

When I entered the lobby, Paco was pacing. He was infectious exuberance, scooping me up into his happiness. I squeezed my eyes tight, wanting to hold onto the moment.

"We've been looking all over for you!" he said. "Thought you might be at the lake."

"I was. Sorry!"

"No problema, hey? We had a good walk! *Cara mia*, meet my friends."

"Your friends?"

"Yeah, the shy Brits over there. Come here, guys, meet sweet Sue."

I twisted in his arms toward the couple approaching me—a lovely woman, but with short blonde hair, and her companion, lithe, but definitely a male, *with long blond hair!*

"Hel-lo. Not shy, just wanted to give you two a bit of space, that's all. I'm Nigel. This is my wife, Nicola."

"So glad you're here, Susan," greeted Nicola, with a sincere smile that meant it. "I need to be rescued from these two!"

"So, okay, let's go!" Paco announced, eager to rouse me. "Are you packed? Let's check out!"

I paused to catch my breath. *Is this for real?* Paco's eyes met mine, "You're here now, love."

* * *

I felt it from the minute the van door slid closed. We left Montreux and began our ascent toward the majestic mountains; an elysian kingdom rose before us. Paco, Nigel, and Nicola reflected back to me what I knew to be true—I belonged.

Paradiso Ultima

I watched Paco, in the garden of his chalet, as he tended his roses, intoxicated with love, the scent of chamomile, and the mountains ringed with clouds. Even the air particles glimmered.

"Maybe you're feeling the affects of the altitude," laughed Paco.

"Don't you feel it?"

"Yeah, yeah, I do," he replied, handing me a voluptuous rose.

* * *

That first night, he had sat on the bed as I undressed, his eyes wolflike as his gaze flickered over my body. I wanted to be beautiful and I felt it, almost. Then, a smirk.

"What?" I demanded.

"You got some wicked elbows on you, girl."

"Oh, I know." I had to agree. "They've got these hook-ey-thingies that jut out."

He folded back the sheet and I slipped in, determined to excel, to be his ultimate lover, and prove just how beautiful I could be.

I awakened sometime in the night, and he was gone. The kitchen was dark, but illumination from about a bazillion stars shining through the windows led to the sitting room. I stepped over the hulk of the sleeping Alfie, positioned to guard the vestibule.

Paco stood behind the desk sifting through papers. Under a dim light, he was pale, his jaw tight.

"What's wrong?" I asked.

"Headache."

"Did you take something?"

"Nothing helps." His voice was soft, but bitter. And I remembered the bullet fragments still lodged and inoperable.

I wanted to go to him, but I could also sense the barrier of chosen solitude he was locked in. So I paused, riveted to the spot.

"They hate me," he spit out, tossing an envelope aside. It fell onto a messy pile of others.

"Why, Paco? How could they? You're so good."

His look, singed with fury, was icy, too. When he finally spoke, his words came out rusty, gaining strength from his anger. He relayed the threats, still current, his fears and his disillusionment. The notorious events of his past that had catapulted him into self-imposed exile were real and horrifying—not the glamorized fodder of the book and film. Ultimately it was his sorrow that filled the room, cracked open the night.

I vowed to myself then that I would love him enough to take away that pain, erase his suffering. Love him enough so he would be free. Free, then, to love me.

* * *

We had hiked since morning, a zigzag path up the mountain with Nigel and Nicola. These big blonde angels had been accepting of me from the first, and within that ease and comfort our bond had deepened. They had an intimate, sensuous contact with nature, quietly pointing out the small things—an elegant insect, a vivid wildflower.

We came upon a meadow of tall grasses sloping down before us. We had only briefly paused before Nigel, with a rallying call, plunged into the meadow, the tips of the grass whipping the undersides of his raised arms as he ran. Then he dropped, disappeared from view. Paco set off next, with a loud roar, until he, too, was lost from sight. Then Nicola and I followed, our footsteps beating out the rhythm of the exultant shrieks that rose from our lungs. At the final notes, I also let myself go limp, collapsing into the grass, creating a kind of nest. I lay there panting, undetected. Enraptured, gazing up into a blanket of sky, I felt a silent communion with the others, aware that they, too, were experiencing the same.

A shadow passed before the sun. Paco had found me. *This must be bliss,* I thought.

* * *

"We'll go to Holland and buy wooden shoes," tempted Paco. It was our last night all together in Leysin. Nigel and Nicola, who had been renting a small apartment nearby, were returning to jobs, a life in London. Before long I too would leave for London to commence my studies; Paco, ever restless, and I would make the drive through Germany to Holland and the flat he had already secured in Haarlem, outside Amsterdam. We made a bonfire, lit fireworks, and ate chocolate-covered cherries. How could I bear to leave the sweetness—the salvation—of this summer on the edge of heaven?

* * *

"What are you, a young girl, doing with this man?" the Russian landlady demanded. She drew deeply on the thin brown Sobranie cigarette she held between her ringed fingers, the long pointy nails splashed vermilion that matched the sinister slash on her mouth. "Don't you realize how old he is?"

"No," I lied. Paco was thirty-seven. "I never asked him."

"He should be with a woman his own age."

I spied Paco on the stairs leading up from the small rooms we had settled into below. He joined us, his smile curious and, I thought, a bit anxious. I held out my hand to him. *Who was this bitch, anyway?*

* * *

Two weeks later, we sat on slanted stone steps leading down to a murky canal curving before a giant windmill. I missed the mountains—the land here was flat—but the windmills were enchanting, so much larger than I'd imagined.

"I don't want to go," I whined. I was scheduled to leave the next day for RADA.

"You've got to," replied Paco, holding me even closer.

"But why? I want to be here with you."

"Because I don't want us to be sitting wherever we'll be someday and you regretting that you gave it up because of me."

"I would never do that. Never."

"Yeah, well, you told me it was your dream to go there."

"Yes, but so is being with you."

"That's not going to change."

* * *

Two days later, I was standing in a leotard in a venerable, damp British building, while an Amazon of dramatic proportions led the class in creative movement exercises. "You are a bell swaying in a tower," she declared. "*Clang*, chimes the bell! *Clang! Clang!*" I suppressed my laughter. Couldn't wait to tell Paco! *Clang!*

* * *

After my last class on Friday, I began what was to become my weekly routine, dashing to Heathrow and a flight back to Holland.

* * *

"It's holy," I murmured. We stood close—one breath before the Rembrandt. It was night; we were among the last patrons to reluctantly withdraw from the Frans Hals Museum. In the courtyard, Paco lit what I thought was a fat match. It flared into a brief, bright sparkler.

Later that night, when I stepped out of the shower, I heard music, a high reedy tune. I leaned against the doorframe and listened, while Paco played "Lara's Theme" on the flute.

"Beautiful," I said, crossing the room, kneeling before him. "I'm pretty sure what I'm feeling right now is *swooning*. I didn't know you played the flute."

"I learned this week, to surprise you."

* * *

My time in London became more and more difficult. I was anxious, unfocused. I nursed my longing for Paco over long dinners and talks with Nigel and Nicola. Paco was our dark, bright captain. He exuded a complex force—a charged but elusive current. He had seduced us all. They too missed his presence in their own lives almost as much as I did.

One day I confessed to Nicola over tea, "I just want to be with Paco. Ya know, the whole thing—home, kids."

"But Susan, is that what he wants?"

What an odd response, I thought. I couldn't imagine why he would not. This was love, wasn't it?

* * *

After several weeks, I decided to drop out of the program.

My acting teacher pulled me aside. "What are you doing?" he asked, "You are already better than most employed actors. Don't give up."

When Paco picked me up at the airport that weekend, he slid a silver ring that he had crafted from the stem of an antique spoon on my little finger.

"I'm not going back," I announced.

* * *

Fall in Haarlem was overcast, bleak and cold. The bright tulips in the vase seemed forced. Paco was edgy.

"Let's get out," he said.

We walked to the Black Cat—there were small bars like this on every block, sometimes two—and ordered Heinekens.

"They're real pissers upstairs," muttered Paco. Just the

daily sounds of the landlady and her husband in the flat above annoyed him.

"Why are we here, Paco?"

"Cause we're thirsty?"

"You know what I mean . . . Holland? You miss your garden."

"'Oh, do not ask, "What is it?"' In other words, don't rain on my parade." He signaled the bartender for another beer.

* * *

November.

It was hardly goodbye, but it felt like it, and for forever, as we kissed one more time. Paco had escorted me to the gate at Amsterdam's International Schiphol Airport for my trip back to the States. I had to return to pack up my studio in Cambridge, figure out my visa, take care of biz. He gently released me. "Come on, baby, be a big girl, you'll miss your flight."

I searched those teasing eyes, reaching out once more to touch his cheek, trace the furrows that lined it. *I'm just going back for a while,* I reminded myself. *I'll return by Christmas.* That was my plan.

But when I watched him walk away, and he didn't turn to look back, not once, I crumpled, doubled over, struck to my core.

Descension Glorioso

In Cambridge, the room that had once brought me comfort seemed unfamiliar. The tokens that I had looked on with pleasure in the past were now just graceless objects. Only the small framed oil on the mantle that Paco had given me held any meaning. In the painting, a couple strolled on a deserted beach before a large windmill. Wrapped in a black wool shawl, rolling cigarettes, I studied it, cherishing each nuance of brushstroke. At night, in darkness, I would caress his ring still on my right hand as if it were sacramental, that it could emit its own omnipotence.

It had been several weeks, and still he had not responded to my letters. How could he not know my sadness?

I was displaced, disoriented. I couldn't find myself within these walls. My anxiety swelled. It felt unsafe to be in my own skin. Because of the urge to jump, I became afraid to stand next to windows.

And then it came—so light, the thin blue paper folding in upon itself.

"Susan— This is, as you will soon realize, a 4 a.m. quicky to remind you what a bad guy I am for not writing and to let you know I'm on the move again. I don't know where yet, probably to a different town by the sea. So about your return, it's not the right time. If you want to write to tell me to fuck off, you can reach me at the American Express in Amsterdam. Be happy, you. —Love, Paco."

* * *

The therapist, Dr.Bronstein, paunchy and rumpled in a thick baggy sweater, was more casual than I'd expected given his Commonwealth Avenue address. I was grateful for his easy smile. I told him about my search for love and meaning and how I thought I had found it. How I had never felt more alive. But now, death hovered. What did it matter living anyway? All was lost and, no, Doctor, I cannot cry.

At the end of our fifty minutes, he scratched his head and said, "Look, you could come once a week and we could sit and talk, but I don't think you need that. Your values are straight. I think you're just in a really bad place, and when I'm in a bad place I go to Esalen."

"You mean, as in California?"

"Uh-huh, Big Sur," he said, checking his watch. "Do you want a hug?"

* * *

I had heard about Esalen, the alternative therapy and retreat center founded in the sixties and devoted to the exploration of what Aldous Huxley called "the human potential movement." Heeding Dr. Bronstein's advice, I signed up over the phone for the first available workshop that had space—"How Do You Want To Live?" or "Living Your Life" or some such title, I pretty much didn't care what.

At the airport, I must have looked as bad as I felt, because an attendant asked if I needed a wheelchair.

"Oh, no, thanks," I responded. "If I could just walk alongside the lady in the wheelchair and hold on, I think I'll be all right."

* * *

The Big Sur coastline was hidden, concealed in a thick fog when I arrived. It was late night, but at the gatehouse, a young guy in braids and a rainbow T-shirt checked me in and directed me to my shared room. The complex was quiet and the low-slung buildings simple. The air smelled piney and salty but with a faint aroma of massage oil and yeast. I crept into the dark room, careful not to disturb the lump in the adjacent bed lightly snoring, and, still dressed, curled on top of the thin coverings, until the sound of the crashing ocean waves lulled me into a fretful sleep.

The next morning, I sat crossed-legged on the floor in a circle with other attendees. Some guy was weeping. The workshop leader turned to me and said, "Hey, you, breathe."

I stopped myself from replying, *Hey, dude, I'm a trained actress and singer. I know how to breathe.* But I knew he was right.

It went on like this for days, the others processing their feelings with the workshop leaders, a hip married couple who "honored my space" and left me alone—except for the occasional breathing directives. I felt shut down and repelled by any group sharing. On my own, during breaks, I was careful not to walk too close to the edge of the rocky cliffs.

After the third day, I could hide out in my room because my roommate, a straight, churchy-looking, middle-aged gal from Stockton, had split. Been kicked out! Apparently (even though I was right there, but so out of it I didn't know what was going on) during a group guided-imagery-and-music session, she and the fat guy with the gold chain necklaces, lying next to her, shared some heavy breathing of their own and got into it. Which was not okay, even for Esalen.

*   *   *

Late one afternoon toward the end of the week, I was drawn out of my room by the sound of drumming. On a patio behind the dining hall, I located the source: a group of men beating out pulsating rhythms. As I stood there, mesmerized, the man drumming in the center of the group suddenly opened his eyes. Was he staring at me? I looked away, and back again. Still the direct, piercing gaze. I turned and fled.

My heart pounding as I made my way around the building, I focused on my footsteps. At the end of the path, I glanced up, confused at my direction, only to meet the drumming man, now looming large before me. I was caught, astounded by the sheer force of his being, as well as his ability to materialize like magic before me. I wanted to turn and dash off, but I couldn't.

He stood as if waiting for me. He was well over six feet tall, dressed all in white, except for his knee-high tan leather boots. His flaxen mane was loosely tied back from his high forehead with leather straps and feathers. His blue eyes, sitting above the sharp planes of his cheekbones, were staggering in their intensity.

"How," I stammered, "did you do that?"

"You need to follow me," he said.

"Follow you?" I fought to muster some composure . . . "Ha! Right."

"Did you get what you came for?"

"Well, I guess not . . . No."

He smiled, turned, veered off the main grounds into the shrubs. I followed.

His long, sure strides led me away on a narrow dirt trail, the low brush scratching my bare legs. Deeper still, around boulders, and over a deep arroyo that we—I, most gingerly—traversed on a spare, weathered plank that teetered as we crossed. The forest was spackled with golden light, thick with beefy vegetation. The forest primeval? Surely. A dense stillness penetrated the green buzzing, the clatter of the unseen.

Soon, a clearing, and a small round dwelling. An equally round woman stood at the door, smoking a joint.

"James," she called out warmly, giving me some relief that somebody knew him. And that he had a *normal*, recognizable name.

"Your garden is just like you," James replied. Neat, tiny, impeccable rows of sprouting plants lined her front yard.

We trekked on, resumed silence.

* * *

I heard the waterfall before I saw it, as we emerged from the leafy enfoldment of forest. We halted at its rim. Spray misted my cheeks and eyelashes, showered my bare arms and legs, a welcome ablution, as cascades of the mighty rapids gushed to my left. James, cornered by the bank of earth to our immediate right, pushed open a wooden door wedged into the rising ground. Folding himself to enter, he turned back, held out his hand, and guided me within.

I stood in a cave, its mouth the matrix, which was sealed with a membrane of clear, thick glass, gazing out at a channel, held between two verdant, gaping, undulating hillsides, streaming into the ocean. A setting sun flamed on the horizon; the light, a current of fire, ignited the channel. Then me as well. *So beautiful!* I wanted to turn to James and say just that, but my breath caught on the words as joy seized me with a stab of memory. And then it gripped me with terror.

"I sense fear," James whispered behind me.

"I can't breathe." It was too much.

"It's okay," he said, placing his hands on my shoulders. "You're just feeling. You are not the fear. Breathe into it. Breathe."

But breath was pain.

I dropped to my knees, and the pain became a howl, and still the pain came. Waves of wracking, wrenching sobs. The pain was for all my hurt for all my days. There was no end to it. Pain that had no name. A pain that was from the beginning and always. The pain was breath.

*   *   *

Hours must have passed. The cave was dark and still but for a diffused radiance from candlelight and the sound of the waterfall. I lay with my cheek to the cold floor. James sat cross-legged before me.

"It was an infant's cry at the end," he said.

He talked into the night. I lay there, emptied, letting the words of his stories, with their odd shifts and paradoxes, wash over me. *Parables*, I thought, *he's trying to teach me through parables*. But I was unreachable, registering only his crazy laugh—his mouth, bizarrely contorted, a lopsided figure eight, one corner twisted up, the other twisted down.

He had been silent for a while when I finally roused myself, daring to really look at him and noticing a softness around his eyes, the skin lightly freckled. And I could see that he was also just a man, and I could sense his lust. But raw with spent emotion and drained with fatigue, I wasn't about to climb the ladder leading to the bed behind him, covered in fur, hanging by chains from the rock ceiling. At least, not that night.

He agreed to take me back to my room.

* * *

When I awoke the next morning, I had no recollection of how I'd gotten there. My mind raced: What had happened to me? My hands gripped the sheets on either side of the narrow bed. *Stop it! Stop thinking! Breathe, just breathe . . .* I tried to relax, breathed in deeply, let the breath flow down, fill and expand the hollowed-out places. Inhale. Exhale. Opened to the breath, building and releasing. And over again, building, stronger. Surrendered, I moved with the breath, becoming one rhythmic, looping motion . . . Then a shift—*thrust beyond*—as I was rapidly propelled through a pitch-black tunnel. Words that I couldn't make out, white letters flashed by. My breath gathered, drove me forward, toward and then into what I *knew* were two aspects of the same inherent power: the bright face of God above and the Dark Lord of the Underworld below. An orgasm, powerful like no other, engulfed my whole body, exploded through my entire being with its consummate force. Immediately I *understood* in mind, body, and soul the simple, magnanimous truth: All life is a cycle, an ever-eternal cycle.

Returning to myself, I was trembling, vibrating. Humming with laughter, a rarified joy, I leaped up, darted out of doors to greet this new day. The grass was moist beneath my bare feet, the chilled marine layer awakening like a baptism. To my left, a lama in orange robes sat in meditation. To my right, James, leaning against the gatehouse, played a recorder.

I walked to the edge of the cliff, the great sea before me.

Standing there on the cliff at Big Sur, bowed by the surge of the elements around me, stripped of artifice, purged of identity, I perceived with awe, I knew with clarity: Nature has the power, not man. It was extraordinary; it was simple: the turn of the seasons, darkness into the light of day, birth and death—an eternal, cyclical force.

I went to James that night, my last, up the ladder, to his bed. His lovemaking was creature-like—succulent, guttural grunts of enjoyment—while I, lying on the soft fur beneath him, the offering.

The Nature of Power

....

Cambridge.

The challenge now was to return to the world.

Nicola's letters were the opposite of Paco's lone sparse offering; hers were grand occasions—bulging envelopes filled with elegant strokes laid upon layers of delicate paper. I looked forward to one as I would a rich, delicious pastry. When I returned from California, one such letter awaited me.

Bemoaning the frustration of finding accurate words to say exactly what she meant, she began:

> *Dear Susan,*
>
> *. . . Words can be so slippery, especially when the person you're trying to communicate with is dearly loved, thousands of miles away, and feeling very sad. It's hard*

*to know what to say about Paco, except that he's, as
always, sad and unsettled. Alfie, too, seems out of sorts.
Probably what they both need is the mountains and
the good air again in Leysin . . . It was hard for Nigel
to draw much from Paco concerning you, when he was
over in Holland. The remark worth remembering is
that when Nigel said, You know you won't find anyone
else as good as Susan. Paco replied, Oh, to be sure, I
know I won't. And it's clear that he really respects and
values you. It's our guess that Paco really feels inferior
to you. You know, it could just be the reverse situation
to the time he asked you to go to Switzerland with
him, and you knew you weren't together enough to go;
perhaps at this time he just feels that he isn't together
enough to be with you, at least he seemed to hint that
was the case . . .*

It seemed unlikely, considering I was the one who had felt
the need to edify my goodness to match his. But a small spark
of hope was lit. It lodged just beneath the constant ache in my
heart. Would he "get it together"? What was I supposed to do?
My dreams had crested and shattered. It was all I could do to
remember to breathe.

Given my experience at Esalen, I expected that I would
come back with a fresh perspective and a healed heart. But,
unable to sustain the high of the communion with nature I had
been graced with, and shaken to the bones of some primordial
authenticity, I felt raw, sober, confused.

I retreated into winter, thankful for the safety of my studio.
Men visited me.

Raul, an actor and director I met when I worked at the
Charles Playhouse, was tough and gritty, wound tight, from the

street. Dangerous, even. But his passion for theatre was magnetic, and past the anger in his eyes was a fierce depth.

I needed to talk. Raul could take it, I thought. I told him about Paco—his story, not the details of our love affair. I still believed in the integrity that drove his passion for truth, justice, a higher good. I clung to it. I found little else to believe in. My fervor was fueled by anger at the people, at the system that ultimately crushed his spirit. What I couldn't acknowledge was that my zeal was also anger at how my life had been affected. I could not allow myself to believe that he just didn't want to be with me.

Raul listened intently, resonated with Paco's bitter struggle as I hoped he would.

But, then, Raul just wanted to fuck me . . . Afterward, I turned away, waited for him to leave. His hot breath on my neck, he wanted more. I feigned sleep. So he jerked himself off, in *my* bed, while I lay there, my face pressed to the wall.

* * *

At six-foot-four and with the added poundage he had acquired in the four years since I had seen him, Drew's massive presence filled the doorway. But his long hair curled below his shoulders, and his lips were delicate, cupid-soft, like a girl's.

"I'm living with a French woman," he said with a shrug. "A gourmet chef."

He settled into the leather club chair, while I sat cross-legged on the rug at his feet.

He had been holed up in New York, he explained, the Village, trying to write.

"Any success?" I asked.

"Naw, it's been lousy. I suck . . . You?"

As we passed a joint back and forth, I tried to put into words my experience at Esalen, describe the wonder of it all, the mystery. I thought he might get it. The glints of affirmation in his eyes hinted that he did. Instead of passing the joint back to me, he grabbed my hand instead, pulled me toward him—a smoky, rough kiss.

"That's not *it*," I said, pushing back. "That's not it at all!"

He looked at me, disbelieving, "How can you be truly free if you can't give yourself to me? . . . Don't you see? You need to be looser to be free."

So I tried. He heaved his vastness over me. My fingers wove into the web of his coarse black curls. I wept and held on.

Out of Innocence

The next time I saw Nigel again was in London, at the bustling and very traditional Dorchester Hotel. It had been three years since our last meeting. He sat hunched, framed in a rose striped damask wing chair, in a corner of the grand room, glancing furtively about, poised for flight. He was armored, opaque, wrapped in a black leather jacket and cap, a black jeaned leg swinging, crossed over the other. His hair was shorn, wintered, his face pale and lined. He nervously fingered a sparse, pointy beard. An eerie portrait of my once-beautiful boy.

I stood poised in the vestibule, on the second stair, hesitant until caught in his recognition. I waved back, animated with the pleasure of greeting my dear friend. Despite his odd transformation, he was, after all, *Nigel*! He sprung up, a cursory nod. Perplexed, and now self-conscious, I crossed to him.

I had come down from Scotland where I had been visiting, with the assistance of a cash birthday gift from my folks, the "sister" town of the theatre where I had been working in Northampton, Massachusetts. The acting, however, proved stodgy and archaic, and, actually, quite incomprehensible given the proclivity toward a rapid cadence which I discovered to be the case throughout the Highlands.

I longed for the ease and familiar intimacy of reuniting with my friends. And well, here was Nigel, but a shocking specter of Nigel. It was if the incandescent luster that *was* Nigel had been sucked out of him. He was so frail and agitated, as if shadowed. As I slowly approached him, it hit me: *He looks just like Paco!* It was all there, the dramatic transformation: The dress, the hair, and, oh yes, there was the pierced earring, but worse—he now seemed to be inhabiting the darkest side of Paco's demeanor.

When I reached him, we embraced, a perfunctory hug. He pulled back quickly, acting as if he were too cool for a public display. "Good, you're here," he said. "My car's parked right out front—quite an amazing feat, actually."

We slowly maneuvered through London's perpetually moist and splattered rush hour in his green Aston Martin. The steady *thwarp* of the frenetic wipers cleared the way toward his flat in Richmond.

"So where's my girl, Nicola? Is she meeting us at home?" I envisioned her preparing one of her lovely, simple meals like we had shared so many times before. Nicola, so warm and inviting, would surely assuage this weirdness. And hopefully shed some light on *what the hell was going on!*

"Ah, I thought I told you."

"Told me what?"

"She's on holiday in the south of France."

When I had called from Scotland, there had been no mention. "No, you didn't tell me. Alone? Who's she with?"

"Not sure, I think with a friend from work. Some bloke."

"Oh, Nigel." The rain's swarm of rivulets tracked the window as my eyes filled with the tears of shock and now disappointment.

"Don't worry, love," he joshed. "I'm really the better cook."

I turned to see him smile then and was grateful for the flash, however faint, of what I remembered as his sweetness and wit. Perhaps just being in real time with each other again is confusing. All this time I had conjured the vision of us together in the fullness of summer: soft, sparkling particles of liquid light. *People change*, I assured myself, *and he's obviously dealing with some tough stuff. We'll relax once we get to his home. We'll get through this awkwardness and relocate what connects us.*

As we entered the flat, Nigel rushed ahead to pick up the ringing telephone. I was just closing the front door behind me when Nigel said, "Here, love, it's for you." He stretched out his arm, offering me the receiver.

"Hello, Nic?" I beamed.

"No, sweetie . . . it's Paco."

Pow! Zam! Just like that, his *voice*—and I was at once *there*—again. *Alive!*

The past days, months, years of separation didn't matter, and everything was Technicolor once more. Vital and exciting. Explosions in the head. Tidal wave in the gut. Zaps to the heart . . . *Paco.*

"Come to me," he crooned. "I have a farm."

"In Holland?" I whispered. *I was there!*

"Yes, you *must* come. Lambs . . . oh, and my garden! I'm talking serious frolicking here." We laughed together then.

"Ya," I teased. "But do you have a windmill? You know how I like a nice windmill."

"Hmm, I'll see what I can do. There's quiet here, Susan, peace. Besides, now is the time."

"I don't know, I . . ." What hold he had on me still . . . And Nigel, who was fairly jigging with excitement.

"Look," he said. "Nigel will take you to the airport in the morning. Just tell me when to pick you up."

"I, yes, all right."

"Tomorrow, then."

* * *

I couldn't eat. We sipped wine and smoked while Nigel riffed on numerology, printing out Paco's name, over and over again, and then *Frank Serpico*, explaining that no matter how you add it up, no matter what configuration of his name, the numbers always added up to 1.

"He's The One, Sue. You're so lucky."

When Nigel dropped me off later that night at the hotel, with promises that I would call him with my flight plans first thing, there were already three messages from Paco. I asked the desk to please hold all my calls. My doubts had begun to surface.

Thus began a night of torment. With the hotel room door bolted, the city's night sky sizzling outside my windows with a silvery luminescence, the war between my romantic fantasies versus some new voice of what—reason or fear? My thoughts careened wildly from one acknowledgement to the convincing other.

How could I not go to him? Here was the man I had loved, that I wanted to give my life to, *wanting me*, wanting me now, offering all I had dreamed and hoped for during these often desperate, lonely years.

Yes, but what about your heartbreak? The battle you endured to find the strength to live again. What about next week, or the month, the year after when he doesn't want you? Can you risk it all again?

HUSH!

I imagined how it could be: the lushness of being in his life again, the voluptuousness of being in nature with him again.

The laughter, the reckless joy. And it didn't matter really for how long. I wanted, no, I needed the *high*.

And now remember the pain of losing yourself. The pain of the crash. The suffering of ruthlessly being dashed into the void again.

But now is the time, he said!

I felt him, willing me to join him. *This could be the right time because he is ready. Ready for us to be together fully the way I want. It could all be so easy, all so wonderful. And if I don't go, I could regret it for the rest of my life.*

* * *

The dawn broke fuchsia and golden. Still in my clothes from the night before, I showered and changed into the long ivory embroidered Mexican dress I had not worn since Switzerland. Had I unconsciously packed it for this occasion? I braided my now waist-length hair with green grosgrain ribbons, packed my bag, and set off for the airline travel office to change my ticket for the first available flight out of Heathrow. The streets were clean and glittering with lemony light. An unusually clear British day.

"Gawd, Paco's been calling me all night!" fretted Nigel. "You did contact him, right?"

As promised, Nigel was driving me to the airport.

"No, I didn't contact him. I'm not going to Holland. I'm going home." My brio did not reflect the fractured dialogue that still raged within. But I knew what I had to do. I knew that I had to save myself.

"But, Sue, how could you? Shit, he'll blame me!"

"I'm sorry for you, Nigel, I truly am."

"What will I tell him?"

"Just tell him: It's not the right time." And I knew for sure then and for always, it would never be.

Still I heard Paco's voice. As if the battle now was not in my head and heart but between *us*. He haunted my steps: *Come to me.* Hurrying through the crowded terminal he called out: *Change your ticket!* Getting to my gate, the torture continued: *I'm waiting for you. Turn around now! Come to me.* When I finally was allowed on the plane, I bolted the seat belt on, squeezing the arm rests. Please, I prayed, start up now. *You can still get off the plane.* Please depart! *There's still time. Come to me.*

"Are you all right, Miss?" asked the stewardess.

"I don't know, I don't know." It was excruciating! I began to hyperventilate. She opened the sickness bag, pushed my head down into it. "Breathe," she said. "Just breathe."

* * *

Great sheets of Atlantic blue stretched out below. Only when the captain announced that we had passed the halfway point did I start to feel safe. And sad as I said farewell forever to the illusion of the fairytale. But also strong as I respected this new clarity emerging. I finally accepted that from the beginning I had embraced each of Paco's romantic gestures as a declaration of his love. But he didn't love me. He needed my youth, my adoration, and my belief in the magic. I reiterated what I now knew to be true: I could not risk giving up one iota of the hard-earned self that I had built these past years without him. The recovery was too important to chance, too difficult to repeat. I was grateful, at last, to put an ocean of truth between us.

* * *

Three months later, Nigel was dead. He had hung himself. Nicola notified me by phone a few days after the funeral.

"He had become consumed with Paco, Susan. And depressed that he couldn't be with him all the time."

It hit me that it could have been me, dead.

"But Nicola, he had you. What happened?"

"Oh, Susan, it got so complex in the end. We . . . the three of us," she stammered.

"The three of you, what?"

"In the bed. Paco's big bed, and . . ." she broke off, sobbing. "Nigel couldn't take it, Paco really only wanted me."

Theatre

Before I journeyed back to London, I had been alone. I had lost my taste for men, for the smell, the heft and exotic thrill of them. For the rancorous expeditions of my heart. After subsisting for many years on coffee and cigarettes, I gained weight, resolutely conscious of that first bite—mashed potatoes—as I layered flesh, actual physical layers, beneath a veil of tender skin. Disengaging from my carnal desires, camouflaged and therefore protected, I presumed I would not be touched, and therefore survive unscathed.

At night, on stage, I performed, taking on roles that forced me to locate strength and power, expressing parts of myself without actually feeling. I played tough girls, like the outlaw Belle Starr, Queen Titania, and Kate, the shrew, even God in an original musical. I could inhabit the essences of these women without being overwhelmed by my personal emotions. My days, however, lacked persona: I was fetal and groggy, disconnected.

Mostly, I slept and read, nibbling on the slices of truth discovered in the books of Carl Jung, astrology, Eastern philosophy. I found credence there for my experiences and a plausible suggestion that there could actually be meaning to the patterns of my life, that it wasn't just a series of random events. This new world of the psyche and soul was intriguing territory and resonated to something deeper in my unconscious.

After Nigel's death, and terminating the grip romantic illusion had on me, the dreams came. Dreams I was dying as my family reached out to me and I slipped into a dark abyss. Please don't go, they pleaded, we love you just the way you are! But you don't understand, I'm dying! In another dream I witnessed a full moon collapse and explode, and a voice, Death is now! Now is the time! Oh no, I thought, now there will be no moon to control the tides. I will drown . . .

Something continued to keep me aloft while being submerged, and although the self I knew was ebbing, slipping away, an integral substance of vitality was growing—incubated in a compelling womb-like texture of safety, filled with graceful strokes of air, breath, and movement. As the days went on these elements began to collide with my nights of pretending. I was slowly turning inside out; I was waking up. But the conscious realization of that still clung to a *me* I could identify. As the yearning for this intangible new grew more compelling, I became more and more dissatisfied with the artifice of theatre. I was terrified, however, to let go, to risk surrendering into the emptiness of the void. Except for my past pursuit for love with men, which I had failed at, being an actress, a performer, was all I knew, all I knew I was good at *doing*.

And then the play came that would write me out of the theatre, change my life forever.

* * *

My brother Edward had matured and pursued theatre with focus and driven industry, committed in a way I never was. He was an accomplished actor and director. I adored him. In all those years, we had never worked together until that summer he asked me to join him in a fledgling company producing a new play by the writer Don Nigro. *The Curate Shakespeare As You Like It, (Being the record of one company's attempt to perform the play by William Shakespeare.)* told the tale of a struggling group of actors who have lost all their leading actors—one to drugs, one to professional wrestling, one to insanity—but were being urged to perform nonetheless by their director (who boasted an uncanny resemblance to Will Shakespeare). When the bedraggled group arrive onstage with their assorted battered trunks full of costumes and props, they realize that they have to go on despite there not being an audience. *There's nobody out there!* The bit players are forced to take on the leading roles and, subsequently, through acting *as if* they are those main characters, they transform. All except for the original Rosalind, my part, who has decided she cannot, will not, say her lines any more, that she just wants to talk to the Curate and the audience—that only she can see. *Rosalind is crazy!* She introduces the scenes, sings the songs, and comments on the action. When bedlam ensues at the finale, when the actors believe their efforts have been in vain and they have given up their faith and are *ashamed*, it is she who emerges from the darkness and delivers the Seven Ages of Man speech:

All the world's a stage, And all the men and women merely players . . .

With each performance, through merging with the freedom of Rosiland's expression—no longer having to say the scripted words—I found myself connecting to a realization, opening to a channel of illumination that I longed to send out to the audience members, to really connect with them *as myself.*

In the midst of these shifting worlds, Chrissie Degas, the ingénue who played Audrey who had to step up and portray Rosalind, the role crazy Roz had abandoned, *kissed* me! Not just some sensitive sisterly smooch, but a full-on, open-mouthed, tongue-searching, I'm-comin'-on-to-you kiss. I was stunned, but, oddly enough, not repelled. I was *letting* her kiss me. Neither of us were gay; at least, I was sure I wasn't, and certainly the way Chrissie outrageously flirted with the guys in the company, I would have thought—if I ever even had a thought about it—that she wasn't either. The male actors and crew *all* wanted her. I knew this from their lech-y stares and the way the atmosphere was charged with their lust whenever she entered the room. And she knew. Played them. Wore shorts cropped to her crotch and tight little tops over her double Ds. But she had no use for them, left them horny every night, riding off after each performance with the Filipino busboy from The Bull Ring, straddled on the back of his Harley. Even I had to admit she was hot.

At the beginning of the season, when I first met Chrissie at the cast meet and greet, I managed to mention the planets, Jung, and past lives all within the first five minutes of our introduction. When I paused, she took a swig of beer, said, "You gotta really cop some attitude to believe that shit."

I had continued to live like a monk, still deliberately celibate. However, by the end of August, my reserve was shaken, my identity discombobulated, and thus I reacted. *Who am I? How do I navigate out of this?* I was boarded in an empty room, save for a single mattress on the floor, expected to rehearse six days a week and perform each night, build costumes and clean the lobby bathrooms—all for a pittance. The night Chrissie showed up with a six pack of Dos Equis, I have to admit, I kissed her back.

"I've never done this before," I managed to confess.

"Are you shittin' me? Hell, woman, did you miss the seventies entirely?" she asked, making no sense to me at all. Yet she sure was adept at shutting me up, blowing my cool, and making me feel better than I had in a very long while.

Although *it was weird*, there was something sweet and revelatory about our affair, as if I was merging with and assuaging the young, wounded girl of my past. The one I had outgrown.

* * *

With the season's climax, I returned home, knowing that I had to leave the theatre, and that the girl I and my family had always known—not only my persona but also my intrinsic self that *was*—had ceased to be. That my yearning for transformation, no matter what jumping off beyond the footlights into the abyss of my unknown future would bring, was tantamount. At the time, I dreamed that I was in a building that was crashing down all around me. As I ran out to freedom, to find my car in the parking lot, I realized I had left my vehicle in another place, recalling an ivy-covered building, a place of higher learning. An old man with a cart arrived and told me he would take me to it. As we rode on, my parents loomed in front of us like giants. The old man offered them money for the honor, he said, of assisting me, and they moved to the side and began shrinking. As we turned a corner, a young man cloaked in the garb of a Native American warrior was waiting for me. I noticed then that I had on the matching feminine outfit. We joined hands ecstatically, knowing we belonged together. We turned and walked up a hill toward a radiance.

So who was emerging? In the past I had been willing to risk all for love; could I now risk all for my Self? Jung and others called it the search for meaning, for wholeness, for spirit, for God. Perhaps, all true—but it would be the Goddess who would come to claim me.

Priestess

....

To our left, a great owl descended, majestic wings unfurled and flapping. To the right of the road, a noble deer darted out, gazing back elegant eternity. Then as quickly, they disappeared.

As startled as I was, Peg, Edward's girlfriend, struggled to steer the van straight ahead, keep it from skidding on the ice. Merely ruts marked this narrow passage through the deep Vermont evergreen forest. We had been lost for hours, trapped in the mountains. We were chilled, weary, and hung over. Searching for courage and warmth, we had consumed two too many Irish coffees at an inn when we crossed the Massachusetts border. Now night was looming, but the apparition of the creatures seemed a greeting, perked us up. Sentries? We locked eyes, exchanged a quick acknowledgment. Yikes! Maybe familiars for the psychic we had kept waiting for near two hours? Suddenly, curled into a sharp bend on our path, Peg's van stalled to a halt.

Before us, lit by an errant ray of waning sun, stood a white Cape bungalow on a silvery knoll. We had arrived.

A young woman greeted us as we stepped into the homey kitchen where a fire sizzled, a pot simmered, and a boy, about eight, clutched a pencil, intent on his book and papers before him on the table. It was all so cozy. So *normal*. Relieved, we babbled about incomplete directions, the weather, and delivered profuse mea culpas.

The young woman was serene. "Yes, you're very late. I'll have to check with Sarah if she can still see you." Noticing our confusion, she clarified, "I'm her assistant, Hope."

Oh, no! This sweet girl isn't her? I was afraid the psychic would be an imposing witch. Damn. Why'd I ever let Peg talk me into this?

I'd had my experience with witches. For too many years the nuns had swooped in and swallowed my spirit. Then I'd kept their dark shadows at bay until the fall of 1975, when Carrie signed us up for Witchcraft 101, at the Harvard Extension. Come on, she'd encouraged, it'll be fun! We jabbed and kicked each other under the long table we were seated at, tried not to laugh, when The Witch of Salem, our teacher, approached in long, black, heavy garb, reminiscent of every Sister-Mary-What's-Her-Name I'd feared. Yet Laurie Cabot was *for real*. And totally not into our humor or nonsense. Soon we were donning black attire, counting down to alpha level—*where all thought is correct and right, so mote it be*—and making projections which, for us, mostly meant crossing our fingers to attract perfect parking spaces. We became *serious*, until the night we sat, in my studio, hunched over candles and incense, marking parchment paper with ancient runes, calling upon the elements, willing the forces of nature to bend to our power. We were enraptured, heady with the mojo, when I first felt a wet drop plunk the crown of my head. We became quickly sobered, as liquid rained down upon us from the ceiling above, sputtering out the candles, smoking the frankincense and myrrh, and splotching our mystic writings. WE WERE FREAKED.

Within days, the Board of Health tagged my domicile unlivable: a plague of water stains, damp, and, worst of all, creeping creepy bugs, including cockroaches. Not the landlord, nor the inspector, could explain the flood. The apartment above was mysteriously untouched.

At our last class, we regaled Laurie with our dark adventure. She laughed, at first, and then narrowed her stare, her kohl-rimmed black eyes warning and threatening at the same time. "Do not ever assume to play with nature, again," she warned.

Chagrined, I acquiesced. But I didn't want anything more to do with the craft anyway.

"Besides," she tossed off, "I'm sure there is a logical explanation. *You* don't have the power."

And now here I was in Vermont again confronting psychic woo-woo. Not my own, of course, but although I was curious, I was apprehensive. Wasn't the act of allowing someone else access to my psyche risky, because I knew that there were realms of nature and magic and power that I had no control over out there—and despite Laurie's protestations, in myself?

* * *

"That's okay, I'll see them. They've come such a long way." The woman who spoke stood in the doorway leading out of the kitchen, into an inner vestibule, softly lit. And she was very pretty. No rueful, scolding hag wrapped in a voluminous shroud. She was about thirty, tall and slender, dressed casually in jeans and a lilac turtleneck sweater. Around her graceful neck hung a silver chain weighted on her chest with a circular stone captured in a cage of silver spokes. She crossed to the boy, stroked his cheek, asked, "How's it going, buddy?"

"Ergh," he shuddered.

"Don't worry, baby, you're getting it."

At that point, a man, carrying a load of wood, swept into the scene. "Hey, Dirk, chilly out there, hon?"

"Oh, yeah," he replied, leaning in to receive his wife's peck.

I want this, I thought, surveying the family scene. *All of it.* It had been a long time since I thought in those terms.

"All right, then," she concluded, her gaze searching mine, "let's do it."

Relieved, Peg made a dash for a chair by the door, perched, and tightly curled one leg around the other. "Yeah, you go first, Susan, I'll wait right here."

* * *

As she became settled, seated by the woodstove, Sarah rocked slowly, then rapidly, her eyes closed, her voice clear but quick, praying, invoking her Guides, Higher Truth, the Ancestors, and Supreme Clarity. She welcomed access to the akashic records where All is written. Seated across from her in the triangular room facing her at the apex, I felt transported. Her words were soothing and mellifluous, lifting me up and carrying me upon the strains of melody. The resonance became recognizable as if she were spinning my own particular soul's melody. And as the notes dipped and flowed between us, my song interwove with other rhythms, then rose as if harmonizing with the rhythms of the universe. Wondrous.

In perfect flow and pitch, Sarah's voice deepened: "There is a woman, older with glasses, in the Washington, D.C., area, playing the violin, who sees you and welcomes you. She will teach you healing through music, color, and symbols. Your life will never be as it's been. You have just concluded a karmic cycle of approximately twenty-eight years. You will now become who you are meant to be, and you will know this . . . In approximately two more years you will meet a man . . . He has been waiting for you. Your true soul mate. In fact, in February, 1981, I see this recognition of your bond. There will be great obstacles to your partnership, but they will be overcome by even greater love . . . You will find a home in the Southwest and welcome a child . . . And together you will all build."

* * *

By Spring I was accepted into graduate school, in Baltimore, majoring in Developmental Psychology, and scheduled to begin an internship with Dr. Helen Bonny, who I discovered was the bespectacled, violin-playing director of the Institute for Consciousness and Music.

Temple Time

Baltimore was sweltering on a Saturday evening. I checked into the downtown Hilton, the Chevette crammed to excess with my stuff—the seen and not seen—not knowing what to expect, except that it was right. I was to commence my training at the Institute on Monday, boarding in a dorm at the College of Notre Dame.

Sunday I explored, following a parade of folks heading to a plaza adjacent to the hotel. An enormous fountain at the entrance erupted before us, shooting off towering green sprays announcing the Irish Festival. Merry tunes called out, sweeping me into a crowd swarming a central stage. Although I did not recall ever hearing the likes of it, I instantly responded to this Celtic music. I grew up with "MacNamara's Band," and such other commercial ditties, in Boston, and only on St. Patrick's Day, except for when my dad, in his cups, tearily reached for the high notes of "Danny Boy." This was different: jigs and reels,

145

gleeful and plaintive. And the drum—the bodhran—was haunting, kindling a reclamation of perhaps some long-ago time. I drifted toward the stage and the silky-haired, green-eyed man (I was that close) who wheeled the bodhran so. I would remember him and his tunes.

* * *

But first I would know the women of the Institute. If it was Sarah who had opened the portal, it was the women at the Institute for Consciousness and Music who welcomed me inside. I had not known such women. The soft, strong embraces who regarded me just as I was: *present.*

The music also enfolded me, stroked the deep remembrances, the questions, the fragments of disturbances that longed now for healing. The feelings long gestating could safely be given voice and understanding.

It was the women and the music who acknowledged me.

Helen Bonny had developed the technique of Guided Imagery and Music (GIM) through her research and experience at the Maryland Psychiatric Research Institute. The application involved individual and group sessions listening to specific taped classical music arrangements, designed by Helen. Simultaneously with my master's psychology courses, in a vintage Victorian, where the Institute was housed, I received a series of these, as an important tenet of learning the process was experiential. Although I had sessions with Dr. Bonny, my main facilitator was Marilyn Clark, the director of the Institute. This was an organization run by women, and although the roles were delineated, it did not feel hierarchical; it flowed, like a spiral.

Marilyn, like many of the others—although they practiced many religious faiths—exhibited, as I would soon learn, a realization of the sacred feminine: strong, wise, nurturing, sensual, deeply intuitive. They were partners to men and women, mothers, educators, therapists, and consecrated to healing. I wanted to be like them, reach those ideals in myself, and therefore I vigorously committed to the work that was necessary.

I realized that I had undergone an ego death, a period punctuated by my leaving the theatre, which also felt like my family and the self they and I had always known. During that time I also came to understand that by accepting, by going through the wounds, I could experience rebirth.

A particular session with Marilyn described my deep feelings as I processed my psychological separation from my past involving psyche and soma:

(The parentheses are her questions and notations.)

I am on the pinnacle of a high mountain. Room only to stand on the top. Looking at a vista, arms outstretched. Bird trying to knock me off. Huge beak.

(Do you know this bird?)
Image of a witch. Afraid. Now a nun, I don't know who.

(Can you take closer look?)
Oh, shit, it's my mother.

(How do you feel?)
Sad. So very sad.

(Can you let yourself go with the feeling?)
Sad, because I have to let her go.

(Anything you'd like to tell her?)
Yes. I'm sorry. Hope she can free herself too.

(How does she receive that?)
She's not able to receive the truth right now, but she may know.

(What experiencing?)
Leaving her at the top of steps. My fear of letting go is not accepting my complete aloneness, separation from my whole family. It's all I've known. Till now. I'm doing it now.

(Where is the music taking you?)
I feel real separation. Have to let them go. Perplexing. Do I have to lose them as people also? Do I need to do it totally? Or go to another level of consciousness?

(How do you feel about this perplexity?)
Like I have to totally let go for a while. So I can breathe.

(Can you do that now? Allow the music to help you do that. How does it feel?)
It feels terrifying and exhilarating.

(Crying.)
I want to say, "Let me go."

(Say it.)
Please, please, let me go!

(Body want to say it too?)

(Forceful breathing.)
(Breath helping you let go?)
(Are they able to let you go?)
They don't want to.

(Do you need to tell them why?)
I don't want to hurt them. Oh, it hurts so much.

(Hands on stomach, then between breasts.)
(Still a lot of pain there?) (Not responding.) (Can you tell me?)
Mixed feelings. Pain of leaving. Hurting them. Worse though if I hold on—I'm doing it, really doing it.

(Now?)
Yes.

(How?)
I'm pushing my way out. Head feels free, feels good. Rest of body coming out—but pain and fear. Where is my strength?

(Where in your body?)
Energy in abdomen. See, it can spread out.

(Concentrate on your abdomen for a while before you move it . . . Bring it up your body now? . . . Push, bring it up to your shoulders and push against this pillow . . . Can you feel it coming up your body? Feel it coming up and out.)
(Holding self.)
I have to love myself.

(Let yourself cry. Any words?)
I can love myself.

(I thought so. Wonderful . . . Can you forgive yourself?)
Yes.

(Is there more to say?)
One part of me—I love you, it's okay. Another part ashamed to say it. But I do love myself.

(Say it all, again.)
I do, I do. Feeling I need approval to love myself.

(Who do you need it from?)
I need you to tell me it's okay.

(I think it's wonderful, more than okay. First step before you can love someone else. Not selfish.)
I have to tell me it's all right.

(Yes, it's a further step of independence.) (She laughs.)
(Telling self it's okay?)
Yes. Not to be so silly.

(Or to be a little sillier!)
Love it all, having to love the shit. All right that past has happened. All the fuck-ups. It's *really* all right. To forgive. It's all right to learn how to save my life right now. If I can accept the shit, I can accept the beauty. Allow it. I know it's there, I just haven't felt it. Also, accept being where I am right now. Beginning. Accept not being perfect.

(Accept being human.) (Deep sigh.)
I'm walking to the edge of a cliff. The sky is brilliant. I want to run—I am feeling light and good. Am at a stream. See my reflection.

(How do you look to you?)
Initially, I thought I shouldn't look. Then—it's all right. I appreciate beauty is nature and my beauty too. I am nature. Getting image of myself as I really am and loving that, accepting all of myself is beautiful. Ha! I just went and threw a big bag of garbage over the cliff and walked away.

(Your garbage?)
Yes! I'm free!

(End of session.)

* * *

I came to understand that true transformation exists only when we can face the pain of uncertainty, loss, and even annihilation. However, allowing myself to fully enter into the experience, I could finally and completely see the incarnation of a new way.

Vermont

....

It was coming on Thanksgiving, the view stark. Wintering trees, knobby crones, their skeletal limbs reaching, pointing, poking toward each other. Their gossip rose, *clickety-clack.* The caramel leaves of once-florid bouffants had fallen from slender branches, quivered, expiring on the pavement. Some had been swept into huddling clusters, while others still drifted. I kicked along in their midst, in the wake-up cold of morning chill. Plainstock, Vermont, a Monday in November, 1980.

I had freaked out the night before, stifled and squeezed into a sliver of an overheated motel room, watching *A Star is Born*, the Streisand/Kristofferson version, on the mini black-and-white tube. I came to Plainstock on the faith of Sarah's reading, ready to embrace my destiny: find a house, open a practice, meet and marry my soul mate, and settle in for the rest of my life. But even above the tinny shivers and hiss of the wall heater, even above la diva's trilling crescendos, all I could hear was the insistent indiction, *What the fuck am I doing?*

Still, in the morning, I dressed and headed out. I had certainly taken risks before and knew that after the fall, after the shattered heart and ego, I had risen again. So one more round? And I had Sarah's vision and mystical blessing to boot. She had certainly been correct about Dr. Bonny and all that ensued.

A white-shingled, black-shuttered church presided over the central Green, shepherding its flock of still-sleepy shops. A bawdy crow, her slick blue-black bosom heaving, was doing some jiggedy-jig on the brick edge of a corner building, *caw, caw, caw*-lling out, This is it! This is it! Below her, a sign: Old Colony Realty.

"Good morning!" the woman greeted. Seated behind the desk in the otherwise empty real estate office, she was around my age, thirty, in a tailored tan tweed blazer, a crisp white shirt collar turned out below a bright ginger bob. "Don't I know you?"

"I really don't think so," I offered, pushing back the hood of my long burgundy heather wool cape. Flipping my braid forward, I was in full-on priestess regalia.

"But you look so familiar. I'm Susie?"

"I'm Susan!"

"No way," she laughed. "Maybe that's it. Just a name thing. Anyway, can I help you, Susan? Ever *Susie*?"

"No, never," I answered, way too quickly.

"Okaaayy, then, so what can I do for you?"

"I'm looking for a house to rent. Do you do rentals?"

"Of course."

"Great. I actually just arrived from Baltimore last night. I'm a therapist, and I'd like to work from my home."

"How interesting. I'm sure Plainstock could benefit. What kind of therapy?"

"Way alternative. I mean, I have a master's in developmental clinical psychology, but I'm trained to utilize a method of guided imagery and music. And art therapy, mandalas."

"Manda-what? I'm not really into any, quote, 'New Agey' stuff," she explained, using her fingers to punctuate. "Hey, but my husband is, mostly Eastern stuff, Buddha and all that. You two should meet."

"Um, sure."

"So why Plainstock?"

"This is even more woo-woo, I mean I love Vermont, but a psychic advised me to come here. Even described the house."

"Oh my Gawd! This is a first! So what does it look like?" she asked, fumbling inside a pack of Marlboros, removing a cigarette, and then holding it out in offering to me. I shook my head no. "Whew," she said, lighting up. "It's my last one. So please, sit down, describe, and make my job easier."

"I know this is weird, but she said it belonged to a musician, who lived in New York, and that there is a baby grand piano next to a wall of casement windows. And the trim on the windows, painted green."

Susie gagged and coughed. "Shit, woman. That's my house."

* * *

It was already nightfall, the nebulous sky of a new moon. Great looming firs lined the pitted road twisting into Holloway Hill. I stopped a few times, turning on the light inside the cheapo rental compact, and checked directions, which did not enlighten me one way or another. So I kept on going, rising, deeper into the forest.

* * *

"Susan, good for you! You found us!" exclaimed Susie, opening the sliding door to what seemed a converted antique barn.

"Yeah! Was that some kind of Plainstockian initiation?" I laughed, entering, handing over a grocery-store bottle of Mouton Cadet. "Yikes, what's it like in the winter?"

"Treacherous. You gotta *really* want to live here. We're just renting till spring while our house is remodeled. You can hang your cape here on the hook."

Did I notice a bit of patronizing?

"I was just telling my husband that I met this amazing woman today."

"Thank you." Okay, maybe I just imagined the tone. I turned toward the room, and there, gracefully sprawled at the end of a navy sofa, illuminated by a Tiffany-style lamp on the piano, was the most beautiful man. It was not just that he was physically beautiful, which he undoubtedly was—curly, silver-threaded dark hair, an Omar Sharif's *Doctor Zhivago* mustache beneath his aquiline nose, and gentle hazel eyes. It was more than that: as if in his calm repose, he was incandescent. His own being the source of the radiance.

It all happened in a flash, and I quickly reined myself in, but not before sending up this prayer: *Dear God, please let there be a man out there like this for me!* The moment passed, and he returned to just being a normal guy, in a red plaid flannel shirt and jeans, rising and reaching out his hand in a subdued greeting.

"I'm Greg."

"Hi." I gestured to the piano. "Do you play?"

"No, can't say that I do. We're harmonically challenged here."

"I love jazz, though," interjected Susie, yanking the cork out of the bottle of red.

"She just really loves the jazz pianist over in Hanover. Don'tcha, Suze?"

"Not now, Greg!" she chided. "Let's have a toast. To Susan: Welcome."

Star Route, 1980

I heard the news on the radio, a coral plastic Magnavox planted on the top of the fridge. *This can't be right!* A steaming kettle in hand, I was poised to pour, yet a spasm of shattering disbelief jerked my system, causing me to liberally scald my left hand. *Shit! Shit!* I dropped the kettle back on the stove and spun, as if facing the radio directly would alter my hearing, shoving the already-sassy red welt rising on the skin between my thumb and forefinger in my mouth, pitifully sucking.

"It's done, miss." The man, his face permanently grizzled by soot and toil, his funky hat squished down below the brow of buggy eyes, hulked in the open entrance of the kitchen leading down to the garage and a temperamental furnace.

Vermont was bloody freezing. I was huddled in my chords, sweater, down coat, and boots that I had slept in the night before.

"You all right there, miss?"

I had scrunched down to the floor, leaning against the knotty pine cabinet beneath the sink. *It just can't be!* Icy tears streamed down my cheeks. "John Lennon is dead."

"Sorry, miss."

"JOHN LENNON IS DEAD!"

"My condolences to the family, miss. If that's all, then." He turned to leave.

"Wait! Do you know where I can buy some furniture? Second-hand?"

I pushed off the floor, stretching to click off the news. Since her domicile wasn't available, Susie had found this rental for me, a ubiquitous small white colonial with black shutters, on the crest of a knoll above Star Route, the main drag leading into town. The house was empty save for my tea things and the four-inch foam mattress I had used in Baltimore for GIM sessions. That and other personal tchotchkes and clothing had been crammed into the Chevette, which now sat in the driveway covered by a dusting of snow.

He paused on the stair, ponderously turning over my request. "Hmm, let me think," he sighed, shaking his froggy head. "There is the Yankee Dick-*ah* over on Dunlap. But he's not really a Yankee, ya know. He's from Connecticut."

* * *

Not much later, there was a rapping at the door. When I looked through the glass, I actually didn't see anyone. Again a rap. Opening the door, I gasped, as a diminutive elderly couple perched on the stoop like pixies.

"Welcome, neighbor! I'm here George, this be Elsie." George, with a thicket of snow white hair and apple-cheeked, shoved a foil-wrapped plate in my hands. I would later learn he always wore his signature red bow tie. Elsie was plain, stout and grey: housedress, apron, sweater, and top knot, but her bright charcoal eyes glowed behind clear wire-rimmed glasses. She spoke not a word but nodded effusively. "This is Elsie's angel food cake."

"Oh my, thanks so much!" I turned to place the cake on the counter. "How lovely, won't you come in? I could make tea."

"No, no, we be going now." They scurried off, disappearing into the inscrutable wall of firs.

* * *

I visited the Yankee Dicker, poking about the murky rooms and scoring a vintage bronze velvet tapestry chaise longue with thick dusty bolsters, its busted springs supported with a plank of plywood; a leafy green damask wing chair; a stained oval oak gateleg dining table and two chairs; plus a double-size mahogany bed with an ornate headboard. A quick trip to Boston yielded from the family basement stored treasures: a generous Oriental carpet, etched-glass hurricane lamps, and a round Portuguese marble coffee table with brass legs.

* * *

Christmas. I was alone. First ever, really. My parents had offered a plane ticket to join them in Fort Lauderdale, but I declined. The previous year Edward and I, sipping port on their southern balcony, had promised each other that our next Christmas would not be spent overlooking the neon "Tropic Shores" sign erratically flickering on and off. And for the most part, I was happy to be alone in my cozy house.

My grand investment was a refurbished Vermont Castings wood stove. The back wall of my garage was now stacked with sixteen-inch white pine, commencing a daily 4 a.m. ritual of rising, stoking the stove, and meditating. This Yule morning was no different except that I nodded off, despite the crackle and roar of the fire. I had celebrated a solitary, but hopeful, Christmas Eve with too many rum eggnogs sipped from my grand-mother's crystal. I believe there was an episode of snow angels. So when Sarah rang up at eight alerting me to stay put and not travel to her gathering, an hour north—as it was thirty below out and there'd been reports of car ignitions bursting into flames—I gladly acquiesced.

The view from the living room was startling pristine. Blinding shimmers of brittle light saturated the pasture that spread out on the other side of the empty road. No traffic today. Swaddled in silence, I curled up, languishing on the longue, and slept. Around three o'clock, George arrived with a plate from Elsie: turkey, stuffing, gravy, the works. Again, a merry howdy, then he quickly dashed off. I was grateful for his cheer, and fam-ished. I ate while watching a holiday film on my old black-and-white TV: Bing Crosby, or maybe James Cagney, and a blur of dancing girls, arms and legs swinging. I must have dozed off again, because when I heard the knock and rattle of the back door, the sun had set, the interior walls in shadows. Still in my pajamas and slippers, I flicked on the overhead in the kitchen. I opened the door to find a young man and woman hovering on the stoop, their frosty breath commingled with the chilly dusk, agitating the molecules of warmth within.

"Yay, we found you! We're friends of Kim's from New York."

"What?"

"We're on our way to Stowe to ski, and Kim—"

"Who?"

"—said maybe you wouldn't mind if we dropped him off."

The woman unzipped her parka, and a sleek, green-eyed, young black cat scrambled his way out of the enclosure, hissing as he leapt into my arms.

"He likes you!"

"But I have allergies!"

"Oh, come on, we rescued him from the pound for a commercial we were shooting, and Kim thought maybe he could stay with you for the week, unless, of course, you want to keep him." The horn from a waiting car in the drive was rapid and shrill. The young man slapped a can of feline food on the counter. "Hey, we gotta go. Thanks."

The woman leaned back to set a plastic dish tub on the floor. "Sorry, there're a few deposits. He really is sweet."

"What's his name?"

"No name. Merry Christmas!"

And they were gone into the night.

I was left gingerly holding the cat, who was busy roughly licking something sticky and probably cranberry off my chin.

"So, cat, who's Kim?"

* * *

I named him Magic, gift of the Magi. Predictably, no one returned to claim him. Released from urban confines and possible cat-commercial stardom, he reigned over his countryside kingdom. Slipping out of doors, he roamed, inspecting his wild domain, disappearing to fierce adventures. He would return to my door for evening sunsets that mellowed the feral treasures he laid at my feet: sparrows, field mice. But like other erstwhile lovers, he would not be mine.

Until the fateful evening when his mournful howls flung me outside into the night. With ladder and flashlight, I climbed the tall pine where he was captured aloft. He did his freedom dance, stepping eagerly, then backward, a paw raised but flight evading. *Come, kitty, leap to my outstretched arms!* Our eyes locked, bright green and true blue. He hit the mark, perched upon my shoulder, claws embedded in wool and snow. We descended.

At the darkest hour, our secret not to mention, he padded the fetal ridge of my enfolded torso. Reaching the crown, he paused, kneading auburn hair, flannel, and down, into a crested nest. Weighted there, he slept, a purring corona.

* * *

January brought clients to my den: Music and valiant fires ignited imaginations and broke through steely emotional veneers. We did good work.

There were also a few dinners with Susie and Greg and their friends. Susie was attempting to fix me up.

"So, Susan," she urged. "Tell everyone about your psychic reading, about meeting your soul mate."

"Oh, I don't know."

"Come on, aren't you supposed to meet him here, now?"

"Yeah, but—"

"So," asked Jed, the only single guy in the group. "Any, *ahem,* candidates?" He brandished his glass, preened, and winked. The group snorted and hooted.

As if! I sipped my wine. "Gee, not a one. No, the landscape is quite barren."

Scarlet Letter

Prissy and Miles lived in a handsome yellow saltbox, set back from the Green, dated 1695. Transcendental meditators, they were planning to move to their guru's compound in Iowa and learn to *fly*. They were a trifle nutty, but I liked them, and they had invited us all to a concert at a friend's house, in Rutland, thirty miles away. The friend, also into TM, was hosting the musician and his entourage, Ravi Shankar devotees. I looked forward to it. Yet, as I turned off the ignition, parking behind Greg's pickup, I hesitated—was I ready for all this?

Because suddenly I knew, not a second before, the man I had been waiting for was Greg, and he had been all along. I would say later that it hadn't occurred to me, that the knowledge had been veiled. That was my truth. But now, it was a clear, shattering thought. I tossed my head back in a howl, punching the steering wheel. I was pissed. Angry at God, and all the powers that be. Especially at my foolish, foolish fate. Finally, my soul mate, and he's *married*? It wasn't supposed to be like this. I had worked so hard, been diligent with myself. Prepared. This was to be not just a mind, body, heart connection, but a spiritual merging as well. A true marriage! I'd followed a conscious path. Even felt virgin again. Yes, *virgin*—whole unto myself.

I was even proud of how I had extricated myself before falling into love and heartbreak. I'd enjoyed a sojourn with the Irish musician Seamus while in Baltimore. We had lifted a few pints, sipped Irish Mist together, smoked doobies, and made out in his van between sets in Fells Point bars. He taught me to dance a few jigs and reels at ceilidhs, and he brought me to the brink of tears with gorgeous tunes on the bodhran and the mandolin. But our relationship became one of convivial companions, slipping through the illusion of romance pretty quickly once I learned he was married—however unhappily.

I had trusted. I had been guided. And . . . it was to *Greg*? Was it faith or madness that led me here?

* * *

Prissy opened the door. I paused at the threshold, the dark wings of the stage, and surveyed the room. The atmosphere was charged with sparks of expectancy, the drama already stated and unfolding, the scene shifting as the players awaited my perfect entrance. Enter the Fool, who steps off the precipice, hits her mark, finds her light, ready to play her action out to the end, no matter how absurd.

"Where's Susie?" I knew the script.

Miles sat at the dining table holding a mug, cradling it in his hands. Greg, standing by the granite fieldstone hearth, turned from the flames and said, "She's not coming."

"Is she ill?"

"No, I was just telling . . ."

Please, Greg! Don't look at me like that!

"I told Susie today. We're separating." His earnest gaze found mine. This lovely, lovely man. I couldn't fake it; I'm not that good an actress.

*   *   *

We four tumbled into the Volvo, a cabal of seekers and sinners. Miles steered us toward our destined evening. Prissy nattered on in the front about her Reiki class at the community center in Brattleboro and her newfound ability to read auras. She swiveled to study us in the back, Greg behind the driver, and me, to the right.

"Greg! Even in this dark, I can see you have unleashed energy all around you! If I could just put my hands on your head. What's going on?" she exclaimed, thrilled and daunted at the same time.

Greg raised his arms, turning his palms out in helpless resignation.

"And you, Susan! Why, there's a hot pink radiance in your aura. That's the heart chakra, you know. It means love." Her eager smile melted as her eyes flickered back to Greg and then held the both of us. "Oh."

"Dial it down, Priss," warned Miles. "Dial it down. Why don't you put in a tape."

Some celestial cassette soothed the tension to Rutland, whilst I internally plotted the redeeming vagaries of an escape—perhaps hurtling myself out into a snowbank and being devoured by wolves.

At last we reached our destination, the hallway rimmed with Birkenstocks and Sorels, a small but crowded group buzzing in the living room. Greg and I found places up front to sit together on the floor. Our shoulders touched, arms, knees pressed into one another's. This night, awareness heightened, senses blurred in the amber half-light, the nag champa; saffron kurta and purple dhoti; long-neck sitar, round tabla; cradled gourd, left foot and knee. Brown fingers, metal pick. Raga: Opening the Heart. Swelling, insistent melody. Sympathetic, sweet harmony, spiraling unity. Confirmation with every breath, every pulse. One heart beating.

On the return drive, we held hands, huddled together in the backseat, suffused with the evening's lingering resonance. Back in Plainstock, we bid Prissy and Miles a quick hushed goodnight. The Green was silent and empty. I was poised to flee, or maybe he was, but then he turned and said, "We should talk."

In the cab of his truck, the windshield frost spiraled and dipped, tracing elegant webs. I was shivering from cold or nerves. I lifted my face toward his, our breath commingled.

"I love you," he declared. "You are the woman of my dreams. I knew when you first walked through my door. I've waited all my life for you. I don't care if I'm your soul mate, but I do know I've never felt like this and I know I want to be with you forever."

He bent toward me, a kiss.

"But Greg, it can't be like this. Way too many shadows. I won't have an affair, be your mistress."

"Of course not! You're my queen. My goddess. I'll make it right. Whatever it takes."

Heiros Gamos

....

March 1.

Greg left his home with Susie the next morning, moving in with a guy friend.

* * *

As I watched the afternoon light lengthen and stream through the western windows, affirming spring would return again, Susie's black BMW charged around the bottom bend of my driveway. With accelerated urgency, the car careened up the side of the embankment. The muddy ruts in the grass would persist for weeks, frosting over each night as a remembrance.

I met her at the door. The hurt and anger in her eyes gathered like storm clouds about to break. But I did instead.

"Susie," I sobbed, "I'm so sorry. I was the last to know!"

"No!" she blurted. "I was!" The glass of the slammed door shattered in her furious wake.

* * *

March 2.

At the post office, the attendant smirked, "Do you want Greg LaFortune's, too?"

"No, of course not." I was shaking.

"Then where shall I forward it?" she asked flatly, winking conspiratorially to the person in line behind me. I grabbed my mail.

Were there still stocks on the Green?

* * *

I needed time. Refuge was with my mother, Fort Lauderdale and her apartment on the beach. We drank piña coladas, ate grilled fish, and shopped in the mall where she attempted to buy me pretty frocks to rid me of my hippie garb. Sometimes she succeeded. I walked the beach at dusk after the crowds left: the French Canadians in their Speedos, the freckled sunburnt Irish New Englanders, and the Jewish grandmothers in their 1940s swim dresses. I looked to the ocean of sky, rays of southern light filtering through the clouds. Once during summer excursions to the south shore of Boston, my grandfather had pointed out that the light was from Mary's fingertips. Given that he was not a religious man, I tended to believe him.

Late one afternoon, a compelling awareness urged me away from the beach, prompting me back to the apartment.

As I entered, Mum handed over the phone. "It's Greg, for you."

"Come back to me," he said.

* * *

I flew to Boston the next day, March 17. At Quincy Market I bought a corned beef brisket and some Guiness and drove the two hours to Plainstock. Greg met me at my house in time for dinner. He never left.

* * *

April 18.

The day began with the routine I had become accustomed to: Rise at four to get the woodstove going, meditate, and then slip back into bed before Greg woke. This morning, however, was Easter Sunday, and my parents were in town to celebrate their wedding anniversary. We were scheduled to attend Mass together and then brunch. They were staying across the border, twenty minutes away, in New Hampshire, at the Hanover Inn. They had met Greg at dinner in the Inn's dining room the night before. It hadn't been pleasant. After a couple of Manhattans my dad became silent and sulky.

When Greg excused himself after the entrees, my father raged, "He's an Eye-talian carpenter, for Christ's sake."

"Shush, Xavier. Please don't raise your voice," cajoled my mother.

"I don't give a goddamn."

"Daddy," I intervened, "he's a contractor, and he's French."

"Worse!" he snorted.

"We're in love."

"Yeah?" he leered, "Well, when the rent is due, the love goes out the window."

"He's very handsome though, Xavier," chirped my mother.

Of course, they still didn't know that he was *married*.

After dinner, my father said a perfunctory goodnight and

retreated to their room. Mum asked Greg if she could steal me for a minute to accompany her to the powder room.

"Of course, Eleanor. See you tomorrow. I'll go heat up the truck."

Mum grabbed for my hand as she watched him exit to the lobby.

"What's up?"

"Before we left to come up here, I had a call from Frank Serpico. He's in the states, and he was looking for you."

My heart thudded. Not in a good way. "What did you tell him?"

"I told him to leave you alone, once and for all. That you're happy now."

"Thanks, Mum," I said, hugging her. "I am."

* * *

I settled myself on the cushion before the warmth of a resurrected fire igniting in the womb of the cast iron. As it took hold I resisted the urge to open the singed door, imagining instead the flickering flames as they caught and roared. I began my meditation ritual focusing on my breath and tried to clear the lingering remnants of patriarchal noise in my head. Strangely, another Voice rang out, lucid and clear: *Stay out of churches*, it said. *Celebrate God and life in nature.*

So I did, canceled our plans, remaining in the sacrosanct chamber that was our love. Because it was blessed. Because it was holy. We both knew. We made love that morning bathed in sun and fire and spring. In the thrall of climactic union, a light rose up my spine, settling in my heart. Everything within and without dissolved to white light, and I *heard* the rapturous sound of *Alleluias*! I *saw* a choir of golden beings who I *under-*

stood to be angels. From the center of this multitude emerged a female figure, illuminated in blue, who handed me a baby.

Sweet minutes passed. I lay quivering. Before he drifted off, Greg's eyes radiated ecstasy and timeless tenderness.

But then all I could think was: *I can't have a baby now! This is* not *the right time.* And then the Voice: *What if Mary had said, This is not the right time?*

Leap of Faith

....

Magic-kitty would now disappear for two, sometimes three days at a time only to jauntily appear smelling strongly of the attar of roses and the stink of salmon, which would send me reeling to the bathroom. He would still greedily devour my dinner offerings, however. Greg said he was double-dipping.

Then he stopped coming home at all. We were leaving Vermont. Greg had built a camper shell for his truck, and I would deposit my car in Boston. We didn't know where we would eventually land, but we thought we would explore the Southwest. Neither of us had spent time there, and we were eager for new horizons. We were prepared to find our place. I was ten weeks pregnant.

The afternoon before our departure, I hiked up the swell behind the house through the firs, a stand of birch and maple trees, and into the thicket of opaque woodland: tall pines tightly packed like a platoon of soldiers rigid with attention. There was no path, and my breathing betrayed my anxiety. I gleaned my way through the timbers, most careful of the underbrush. Although I became chilled in my sleeveless shift, I was also sweating as I ascended. At the crest, however, the terrain sloped, and given more light, I was able to pick my way through a copse of smaller evergreens. Soon the aroma of apple blossoms overtook the pine as I was surrounded in an orchard of burgeoning fruit trees. To my delight, a breeze fluttered the petals, and they carpeted the ground and baptized me like confetti at a wedding. I stepped out onto a cushioned lawn of clover edging a tidy grey shingled bungalow. Seated on the porch was Elsie. And Magic purring deliciously on her ample lap.

"Come sit with us, dear."

I joined them, settling into a cane rocker. "His name is Magic, you know."

"Gift of the Magi," she winked. "He's been quite the help around here. George is getting a might too stiff to be chasing the mice."

"Ah, so he's been earning his keep. Perhaps this arrangement can be permanent. Elsie, I'm leaving tomorrow."

She patted my hand. "Honey, you need to get out of here. I know what this place can do to one. I've put up with it for eighty years. You can't help who you love."

"So you know."

"Of course, but you pay no mind." She wiped her moist eyes with a folded hanky, shook her head, and sighed. "You know, I grew up here, but many years ago I left to attend nursing school in Boston and stayed on to work. I had always wanted to live in the city—the rural life was not for me, I'll tell you. My parents were both deceased, and my only sister was married—to George. But when my sister became ill, I returned here to care for her. When she passed away, I stayed on with George. That was fifty years ago, and the town still goes go on about it."

Southwest

....

If Vermont was the frostiest and greenest, New Mexico was its opposite. Stretched out on my back, my feet out the passenger-side window, I rested my head on Greg's thigh as he navigated the blacktop. No air-conditioning. Cactus, clouds of brown dust, and tumbleweed flew by. We could've been on another planet for all I resonated with the arid terrain—seemingly blood-stained from the brutal epics of other travelers. In the vast exposed wildness, copper-hued sandstone rose like crumbling monuments, some topped off with jagged boulders coned like dinosaur teeth. Dark passages furrowed into the striated rock sides of mesas or buttes. *What's the difference?* I did not care. At the last stop for gas and breakfast, cowboys ate while still wearing their hats, for lord's sake. No, I did not want red *or* green chile on my eggs, thank you very much. Outside, a bony horse seeking shelter under a sliver of shade shuddered and twitched from the flies.

We chose this area because it was new to us both, no lingering personal history. New life, New Mexico, we joked. And a new name for me. The morning we were leaving Vermont, Greg had awakened with a dream. "You had a different name, A-l-e-x-i-a," he spelled out. I was relieved for a different moniker. Every time he said my name, I heard *Susie*. *Susan Doherty* slipped off easily, evaporating without a tug or a whimper, as if it had used itself up, hit its expiration date. *Alexia* felt stronger, held me like a carapace, a shield.

I did not know this place. I did not like this place. The Land of Enchantment? Too hot, too bright, too dry. My nature reveled in my fecund origins: moist broad lawns, tangled English gardens, old oak forests and the undulation of seas. I was broody, needed a home. I was about to play out the most significant role of my life: mother. Where were the women? I wanted Marilyn, the ladies in Baltimore, their kind, wise caresses, their lullaby tones. I missed my mother, even the aunties and cousins chattering, their whooping laughter and brusque hugs. How could my child be raised in exile without a family of heritage? How would my child grow in a barren, rugged habitat, be able to play freely, to skip and run dodging the dangers of snakes and scorpions?

How could the divine feminine find me here just when I needed that sustaining assurance the most? Would Greg and I also be cut off from the genesis of our love? Could we survive this stark blazing reality? My alarming revelation: I was lost in the desert with a man I barely knew.

And what about him? Did he harbor regrets? He'd left not only a marriage, but also his ancestral New England roots, a home, a business, and friends who had, indeed, all abandoned him. He was burdened with a mere mortal, hormonal woman, prey to morning and car sickness, with swollen ankles and tender breasts, leg cramps and fits of weeping. Surely no longer the goddess of his dreams.

North from Albuquerque, Santa Fe appeared to float like a

violet island. The surrounding foothills at the base of the Sangre de Cristo Mountains were polka-dotted with pinion and juniper. Lightening crackled overhead in a charcoal-streaked sky, the sun, a taunting, enduring orb. Still no precipitation. I yearned for rain.

In the city limits, we cruised down Cerrillos Road, golden arches, neon chile signs. Basses blaring, low-rider cars jerked and bucked. We circled the main Plaza peopled with tourists in shorts, T-shirts, and ball caps. Inscrutable Native Americans displayed their wares: strings of turquoise and shiny silver. We agreed to keep on going.

Taos appeared authentic and serene compared to the adobe Disneyland an hour south. We checked into a motel, a cluster of low-slung casitas. I had never been so thirsty. We sat by the side of the pool dipping our feet. Greg massaged my calves. We tried to come up with a plan. Should we head back East? Forge on to California? The easiest solution was to go south. We were hoping for a progressive community, support for our work, and, most dire for me, to set up prenatal care.

Days later we had checked off New Mexico—Truth or Consequences, Ruidoso, Las Cruces—crossing over into Arizona. Humanoid saguaros popped up into view, arms raised as if startled in a holdup. Whether through relentless road fatigue or spirit weariness we finally stopped in Oak Creek, adjacent to Sedona. We found a room next to the creek. Water! There was a New Age bookstore and nice hippie folks. Greg was hired immediately, building and installing wine racks for a local restaurant. But a few weeks later the job ended, and there were no others, and we were running out of money. Should we use what was left to rent an apartment with its required first, last, and security deposit?

* * *

I kept the door to the booth open to reduce the wicked heat, dropped coins into the pay phone. *Please, please, please,* I prayed. I had met Jennifer at an event at the Institute in Baltimore, had been drawn to her generous personality and humor. "If you ever get to Albuquerque," she said, "call me."

My story spilled out. I was in Arizona, pregnant, with my mate, and desperate for direction.

"Perfect timing," she enthused. "I'm on my way to the Butterfly Dance at Hopi, which you absolutely must see, this weekend. Meet me there at Second Mesa, and I'll help you figure it out. My husband John actually just took a lease on a casita in Santa Fe for a sometime getaway. That could actually work for you for a while. Okay, great, we'll talk. And when you get to Hopi ask for the banana clan," she laughed. "Actually, it's *bahana*, which is Tewa for *white man*."

* * *

As the late-summer sun rose above its tip edge, Second Mesa loomed like a castle in the sky. We ascended the steep serpentine road, passing the ruins of bygone villages. Approaching the mother village of Shungopavi, angular houses merged subtly with the stone. After parking, we followed the deep low rhythms, the singing and rattling, to a central crowded courtyard. Jennifer waved for us to join her. We were easy to spot.

We joined the very few anglos, who deferred to a bearded, not-quite elderly, but certainly old, man seated in their center. He wore the most extraordinary hat with an exaggeratedly tall crown and broad brim. His long grey braids were fastened with beaded strips of leather. After introductions, Jennifer made room for me on the stone wall next to him, Robert, this Frenchman holding court. Greg sat cross-legged at my feet.

In a large circle, facing in, young men and women moved in place, lifting one foot then the other, as if they were respectfully dancing *into* the earth, as a homage. The women's bare feet were painted yellow, their ankles strapped in rows of tiny bells. They were costumed in capes and in black tunics and skirts with rect-angular- and diamond-shaped designs of brilliant orange, red, green, and cobalt blue. Sleek raven black hair flowed beneath magnificent irregular-edged headdresses decorated with feath-ers and symbols: rainclouds, flowers, corn, butterflies. Sprigs of pinion were clutched in both hands.

The men, in white tunics with multi-colored ribbons, shook gourds, shuffling high suede moccasins laced with bells, tortoise shell rattles clamped at their calves. Fur pelts hung and swayed down the backs of torsos.

After a while, I felt trapped. I tried to focus, take in the splendor I was invited to witness. But my butt hurt on the hard surface. My legs throbbed. My skin was no doubt frying and freckling. I had to pee. I could not, however, see a way out. Surely one couldn't cause a scene—a pathetic pale pregnant girl streaking across the sacred space wailing, "I want to go home!" More than anything in the world, I wanted to go home. But even if I could, just where would I go? A sharp jab jolted me from the inside, then, as if to say: Wake up, Mama!

I laughed, perhaps even out loud. Because, of course, there was no exit. Nothing to return to. Useless to struggle. Useless to resist. *The way out is through.* Had I read that somewhere? Another sharp kick, tricking me back to, well, breathing. Ah, yes, remembering to breathe. Does it always need to come down to this? Have I learned nothing at all?

Greg leaned back, his head cradled at my knees, my hands, palms down, on his shoulders. He had been steady and assuring with me since the beginning. My rock. My truest love. Finally exhaling into surrender, time evaporated within the repetitive beat of the dance, the hypnotic drone of the chant, the constant thumping and the pounding of soil into the ground. Allowing myself to be absorbed in the experience, an energetic current entered through the soles of my feet, a force being drawn up from the earth's nether regions, leading me to comprehend: This is where I will now find my strength.

Greg, sensing the charge, placed his hands on mine. We had been carried here by the recognition, trust in and thrust of our psycho/spiritual/heart alliance, but now it was as if we were being asked to ground and bind our union to a physical place. We were in the dawn state, the infancy of a new consciousness, challenged to create our wholeness together.

Hours could've past when Robert tapped me on the hand and Greg on the shoulder. We followed him into what I hoped was the cool darkness of the small dwelling just behind us. I felt dizzy from the sun, stooping to enter the open doorway, certainly not designed for Celtic amazons such as I. Inside, the atmosphere remained hot and dusty—dirt floors and ceiling, the walls exposed mud bricks. A group of older Hopi women invited us to sit and eat.

"The grandmothers," whispered Robert. "Hopi is a matrilineal society. My wife was sister to this clan."

In simple dresses and flowered aprons, the women were short in stature but large and comfortable in their roundness. Detached, avoiding eye contact, yet graciously putting up with us. I could not presume I had any idea what it was like to be Hopi. One handed me a clay cup of cold sugary tea. Then a terra cotta plate of beans and a greyish-blue wafer-thin rolled bread of several folded layers, which Robert named *piki,* assembled from ground blue corn and juniper ash.

"Maize is sacred to Hopi. It represents the Corn Mother,"

Robert explained. "We eat it as a sentient being, like the Catholic host. It becomes your flesh and then mother's milk."

The crisp weightless bread melted on my tongue. I was grateful.

Robert regaled us with his tales. As a profligate young man in Paris he once dreamed of a stunning Indian woman in white buckskins bearing a pipe—White Buffalo Woman—explaining that she appears to men when they have lost their connection to the earth. He set out on his own journey of discovery, ultimately compelled to Hopi. There he was taken in by an elder who taught him about his own manhood and the ancestral teachings of Hopi wisdom. During this time, he fell in love with a native woman. He stayed on studying, learning, and adopting their culture for fifteen years until his wife died. When he left, ready to reenter the world of the *bahana*, he settled in Cuyamungue— the place of sliding rocks—north of Santa Fe, where he again married. He built a kiva, a ceremonial chamber, in his home, where he guided young men in the Hopi ways, helping them to find balance within themselves and harmony with the earth. "The Banana Clan," he chortled.

That night, I dreamed I was in an underground womblike cavern, black as night except for the flames erupting from a hole in the center. This was how we entered the earth, I understood, and returned to it. I too would bleed my life into its source. I felt the developing life pulsing within me, urgent and vital. Our heartbeats resounded, filling the chamber, as one.

La Querencia

Santa Fe.

Perspective shifted, a fierce beauty emerged everywhere. The cloudless stretches of vivid cerulean sky gave way to nights of bazillion stars. Various hues of earthen clay plaster were the perfect complement to display a fuchsia bloom on a cactus, the crisp white lace curtain in a window, potted red geraniums on the sill. A turquoise painted door. September light was softer. The tourist hordes dwindled, returned the city to the serenity of itself. The aroma of pinion fires and roasting chiles filled the air.

Our quest for home had its regulations and timing. Like the alchemical uroboros, the mythical serpent swallowing its own tail, we were required to complete a transformational geographic circumnavigation throughout the Southwest before we could reenter the gates to the city of holy faith. And be welcomed there, pilgrims seeking sanctuary.

We lodged at John's for a few weeks before securing our

own casita dead-ending Gypsy Alley on Canyon Road. Greg was hired by a construction company who valued his interior-finish expertise as he went about learning the indigenous architectural styles of New Mexico.

I filled my days waiting, walking, carefully aware of each step, weaving myself into the atmospheric present and the devotion of Santa Fe's storied past. I had discovered Our Lady of Guadalupe, the brown Queen of the Americas, in the Notre-Dame de Paris. Especially revered here, her image—in her colors of Mexico, red, green, and white, adorned with her signature roses—was displayed everywhere throughout the city, on tiles pressed into walls, on storefronts, car decals.

I learned to cook beans, posole, and blue corn bread from the butch women, hunting knives slung from their waists, who ran the local basement co-op. They were helpful to me as my belly grew enormous, hauling my full bags up the steep staircase to the parking lot.

We found a homebirth doctor who also resided on Canyon Road, and we attended breathing classes with our midwife, Naomi. Our landlord Rudy Rodríguez encouraged us with our plan as his mother had birthed twelve children in this compound, which was once his family homestead. The due date was set for around January 9.

* * *

December 30.

Greg's divorce was final. On December 31, I planned to meet him at the courthouse for our marriage license. John, a universal life minister, offered to officiate at a gathering in his home in Albuquerque.

When I arrived at the registry, the two young women stared at my condition.

"Eeee, where's your fiancé?" asked the fatter one all sarcastic in her big bad permed hair and "wall of death" bangs.

"He'll be here."

She smirked at the puny one, who stared wide-eyed from behind her glasses. "Well, he bettah. We close at noon today." She said something cryptic in Spanish, and they both exploded in laughter.

The clock read 11:50.

With that, my hero ran in, much to the girls' surprise and obvious disappointment.

We filled out forms, paid the fee, and were just about to leave when the puny girl passed a pink plastic bag across the counter. On it read: *For the Bride.*

On the sidewalk Greg gave me a quick kiss before leaving to go back to work. I opened the bag: a Harlequin novel, a small box of Tampax, a sample box of Tide detergent, a mini bottle of Midol.

* * *

Back at the Old Town Hilton, where we were staying for the night, following the brief but lovely ceremony at John and Jennifer's, I called my folks. My dad was so relieved that I hadn't been left on the sidewalk, barefoot and pregnant by some shiftless carpenter, that he wept.

* * *

January 24.

Labor began at 11 p.m. on Sunday. Greg snored beside me while I sat up all night as gentle movement ebbed and flowed. Marilyn dreamed I should focus on the image of a spiral. Robert had brought me a flat spiral seashell to hold. I was serene. I was Woman. *What's the big deal?* By 8 a.m. the contractions stopped. Greg stayed home with me, as we were sure the birth was imminent. We walked to the reservoir on Upper Canyon. The cattails, ducks, and beaver dams were a nostalgic New England treat. I made minestrone soup and quiche for the post-birth feast. Sparkling cider was on ice. I glowed in anticipation. Even better than Christmas. We had spent our first Christmas Eve together arm in arm strolling past the *farolitos* and luminarias that lined Canyon Road, stopping at bonfires and carolers who offered us hot cider. Greg gave me a beautiful woven ruana in indigo and purple yarns. His gift was an alabaster and rosewood ceremonial pipe.

That Monday night, the same routine: 11 p.m., contractions began again. By 2 a.m. they were stronger. I woke Greg and told him, "Call Naomi."

Naomi arrived and checked me, but she assured us we were in for a long night.

She snoozed on the couch. Greg fell back to sleep while I kept vigil. By 8 a.m. all was still again. Nothing. Naomi left to go to the doc's office but would be in touch.

* * *

January 26.

Surely this would be the day? I asked Greg to please put on a white shirt while I wore a white nightgown. I had spent pregnant months only able to eat white foods. We put on a tape I selected called *Golden Voyage*. I was exhausted but too excited to nap. I didn't want to miss anything. My mother called, then my dad, Skip, and Edward, each calling from separate coasts. Greg's sister. Each time the phone rang, I thought it must be God calling to tell me that it was time. Everyone was waiting. I became nervous that something might be wrong. Or perhaps this child just likes to take its time? What was *I* doing wrong? Then I recalled something I had read that said in order to activate the oh-so-necessary oxytocin, maybe we should make out. So we did. My hypersensitive breasts responded, and all of a sudden I was in full-tilt boogie labor. *Eeeeeeiiiiiiii! Wait a minute!*

* * *

The late Tuesday afternoon light was waning. I escaped into the tiny bathroom, called out, "Greg!" I was delirious with fatigue, pain, and terror. I did not think I could live through another contraction. I had to get out of there.

"What is it, honey?"

"You've GOT to help me out that window!" I flapped my hand at the two-foot-by-two-foot glass. Even at my skinniest, I could never have made it through.

"What are you talking about?" His worry was obvious.

"Please, help me! If I can just make it to Mexico . . ."

"Honey. You're. Having. A. Baby."

"I CAN'T DO IT!"

The midwife appeared at the door. "Come on, Alexia."

"I'm sorry, but I can't do this." I waved her off dismissively.

"Alexia, you're doing great. You're almost there."

* * *

4:57 p.m. She was perfect. She was exquisite. A spiral of fine hair traced low on the center of her forehead. We named her Vanessa, a genus of butterfly, a symbol of rebirth and resurrection.

Los Angeles, 2002

I t was an omen. Vanessa's fave guy-star, Ben Affleck, filming on the Pacific Coast Highway. She squealed, Greg shuddered, and I laughed out loud. We were on our way north to Vanessa's final callback audition for admission to an acting conservatory. We continued cruising up the coast under a New Mexico blue sky reflected in the swells of the Pacific. Perfect moment.

Vanessa had hated college. By March of her sophomore year, she was majoring in depression.

"Mama, the only time I'm happy is when I'm acting," she sobbed.

I knew then that it was as difficult for her to embrace the theatre as it had been for me to leave it.

"Nessie," I replied. "At least you know what makes you happy. You've gotta go for it."

"Then it's okay if I leave college?"

"Yes, of course."

"I want to train. I want to be really good."

* * *

Vanessa's theatrical proclivities had been a shocking revelation to me, lulled as I was in my hard-won, peaceful familial existence in Santa Fe. I had diligently and purposely raised her in a nonperformance milieu. The world of the theatre was a faded and long-ago-healed memory. Or so I thought. One afternoon I sat, in a kind of somnolent bliss, amongst other mothers who wear their children like name-tags on their breasts, in a funky adobe basement, taking in a silly after-school play. Then something went dreadfully wrong. My heart squeezed as the roar of my past and present collided. I wanted to jump up, yell, "No! Stop!" My best friend Barbara grabbed my hand. *She* knew? Oh no, it isn't just me! *Everyone* could see what I was seeing: There in her glory, in the center of a tiny ten-by-twenty-foot platform, lit by a couple of tin-can-covered lights, was my daughter, in her eleventh year, a shining star. This quiet, often-reserved child commandeered the stage like a seasoned pro, with confidence and a charming comedic timing. She was outstanding. And worse, she was loving it.

After the final applause, audience comments supported my reaction.

"Vanessa is so talented!"

"She was amazing!"

"We had no idea!"

Neither did I. Nor did I want to.

My emotions were paradoxically complex: a mixture of pride and joy for her sake, and utter bewilderment and horror. It was like some deus ex machina had descended from above, pointed his wicked finger of fate at me, and was laughing in cruel glee.

I was not prepared for this. Never saw it coming. This babe that I bore, that I had intimately groomed and guided, had calmly and magnanimously claimed herself in front of me, her father, and the rest of her albeit small but nonetheless important universe.

Later, we celebrated at a restaurant, her choice, where the waiters served up Broadway tunes with the enchiladas. In the middle of "What I Did for Love," I lost it, tears streaming into my tortillas.

"Mama, what's wrong?" Ness whispered.

Greg placed his arm around my shoulders, pulling me close. "This was a big day for your mother, Ness. She's just so proud of you."

That night as I tucked her in, Vanessa, her innocent face pure in its assurance, announced, "So, Mama, I've decided I'm going to be an actress instead of a doctor when I grow up. I like doing something I'm really good at."

I kissed her, smoothed her brow. "Whatever makes you happy, sweetheart. But you've got a lot of years ahead of you to decide. For now just enjoy being a kid."

After I turned out the light and said goodnight, I made an emergency phone call to my brother, who was directing a show in New York.

"Edward," I cried, "She's an *actress!*"

To which he calmly replied, "What did you expect?"

"No! Never! Not this!"

"It might very well be different for her, sis. Acting is a noble profession, and besides, actors are angels."

* * *

We are in separate vehicles. I'm in the Volvo. Vanessa, driving her own car, follows.

Out of the hundreds that auditioned nationwide for the conservatory's small class of thirty, Vanessa was accepted. Her two-year program of total immersion will begin in a few days. I am exhilarated; surely rays of joy are radiating out of me. It was evident when we arrived at the school for her audition: *This is where she belongs.* She's on her way now, connected to her art, her purpose, and her powerful sense of self that will be nuanced with beauty and luminosity, honed by sacrifice and responsibility.

It feels like another kind of birthing.

* * *

The next morning, we had coffee at Starbucks.

"Mama," she looked up at me from across the table, anguished, wrestling with some internal torment. "What if I can't do this?"

"Then you'll take the next step. Write another chapter. It's *your* story revealing itself, *mija.*"

"Yeah, I guess."

I took her hands in mine, still baby-soft. "Vanessa, everything you need to be a successful actress, artist, woman, you already possess. You *can* do this. You already are."

"Okay." She shrugged, removed her hands, took a sip of her Americano. "Actually, I'm really excited." Her smile was dazzling.

"Oh, thank Goddess!"

She laughed. "But what about you?"

"Argh, I don't know, but I'm all right. Been thinking a lot lately that if Boston was about my soul, then Santa Fe was about my heart. Just haven't figured out this whole L.A. thing yet."

"That's easy. Yourself, Mama. L.A. will be about yourself."

* * *

That afternoon, I cruise down the coast heading home, singing Sondheim, secure in the knowledge: She's launched.

Gratitude

....

In the beginning was the *Word* . . .

* Leah Komaiko and the delightful writers of the UCLA memoir group.

* The Woman's National Book Association, LA Chapter writing critique group, who challenged me, inspired me to work harder, and polished my convoluted prose: Joan Jackson, Lindsay Lees, Christina Alex, Ellen Ruderman, Kim Gottlieb Walker, Jovita Jenkins, Kathryn King Segal . . . and especially Margaret Karlin, who stole my parking place and won my heart.

* My Santa Fe tribe, who stood with me and by me through the years, and who had the good grace to never ask, "Is this the same book?"—Kamala Harbour, Jeff Harbour, Kathleen McCloud, Nancy Sutor, Rosario Provenza, Janna Rapoport, Susan Halvorsen, Steve Halvorsen, Babette Mirabelli, Mario

Cabrera, Delyse Fields, Philip Retsky, Stan Jones, Kirtlye Parker, Jay Cawley, Sati Kohn.

* Barbara Bruneau Cleaver, my anam cara, who dresses and bejewels me, reads every word, tends to my soul, rises with me, and ALWAYS makes me laugh.

* My clansmen and women, the best a girl could have: Skip, Mark, Max, Gus, Lace, Lynne, Hilary . . . our treasure, the queen of hearts, Christina Selian; where would I be without you? And the incomparable, the divine Liz Healey!

* The LaFortune women, Victoria and Stephanie, who rooted me on to the finish.

* Brooke Warner and her team, who actualized the dream.

* Selimah Nemoy, for her sharp eye and sweet soul.

* Amy Ferris, who saw me, shined a light on me, championed me, and changed my life forever.

* My ultimate teacher, the exquisite Vanessa Collett LaFortune, for her patience while I learned how to be her mother and become the woman I am today. Gracias, mija.

* Ultimately, and forever, Gregory LaFortune, the finest man in the land, who sustains me with his enduring love and faith. Siempre te amaré . . .

About the Author

Alexia LaFortune, MA, Developmental Clinical Psychology, MARI, FAMI, is a creative arts therapist, writing coach, and screenwriter. Her personal essays, "Beds I Have Known" and "Hairdo from Hell," have been published internationally. She is in private practice and conducts creativity workshops nationally, including the popular series, "Eat, Talk, Write." She lives in Los Angeles with her husband—and in Santa Fe, New Mexico, as often as she can.

CPSIA information can be obtained
at www.ICGtesting.com
Printed in the USA
FSOW04n1717250416
19668FS